a POCKET ESSENTIAL

SHORT HISTORY
OF THE
VICTORIAN ERA

a POCKET ESSENTIAL

SHORT HISTORY
OF THE
VICTORIAN ERA

GORDON KERR

Oldcastle Books

First published in 2019
by Oldcastle Books Ltd,
Harpenden, UK
oldcastlebooks.co.uk

Editor: Nick Rennison

A CIP catalogue record for this book is available from the British Library.

ISBN
978-0-85730-207-6 (print)
978-0-85730-208-3 (epub)

2 4 6 8 10 9 7 5 3 1

Typeset in 12.5pt Adobe Garamond Pro
by Avocet Typeset, Somerton, Somerset, TA11 6RT
Printed and Bound in Great Britain by Clays Ltd, Elcograf S.p.A.

Contents

Introduction

The Victorian era was the period during which Queen Victoria occupied the throne of Great Britain and Ireland, an era that lasted from 20 June 1837 until her death on 22 January 1901. It was a time of tumultuous change in the country, both for the Queen and her subjects. It was also a time when Britain truly dominated the world. The British Empire, of which she was sovereign, was, at its height, the largest the world had ever seen, covering more than 20 per cent of the earth's land surface and including more than 20 per cent of the population of the world. It reigned supreme in the nineteenth century as did British industry and commerce. British manufactured goods dominated world trade and business. Goods were produced more efficiently and priced more competitively as a result of British technology and innovation. In the textile industry, for example, technological developments caused an astonishing growth in productivity. An unprecedented variety of goods and items became accessible to the new mass market at home and abroad. Other countries lagged far behind which allowed Britain to use its commercial, financial and political power to turn itself into the much-vaunted 'workshop of the world'.

They were extraordinary times that brought changes not only to the economy but also to society. There was massive population growth. The population of England and Wales increased from 16.8 million in 1851 to 30.5 million in 1901, the year of Victoria's death. The population of Scotland rose dramatically, too, from 2.8 million in 1851 to 4.4 million in 1901. Ireland's population went the other way, however, due to the devastating famine that ravaged the country between 1845 and 1852, after a blight affected potato crops. This led to death on a huge scale and mass emigration. A million people died and another million emigrated in search of a better life. Emigration was not limited to Ireland, however. A further 15 million left Great Britain, headed for Canada, the United States, South Africa, New Zealand and Australia.

Politically, the two principal parties throughout much of Victoria's reign were the Whigs-Liberals and the Conservatives, although as the century drew to a close, the Labour Party was beginning to emerge as a force. There were great statesmen, some of whom held the highest office in the land on more than one occasion. Amongst the great men of the age were Lord Melbourne, William Gladstone, Benjamin Disraeli, Sir Robert Peel, Earl of Derby, Lord Palmerston and Lord Salisbury. The weighty matters with which they tussled during Victoria's reign included electoral reform, the Corn Laws, factory conditions and Home Rule for Ireland.

One of the most important changes that occurred in the Victorian era was undoubtedly the extension of the electoral franchise. In 1780, just 214,000 had the right to vote in England and Wales – a mere 3 per cent of the population. It was worse in Scotland where only 4,500 men – out of a population of 2.6 million – had the vote. Large cities such as Leeds and Birmingham did not have a single MP to represent them, while 'rotten boroughs' – constituencies with tiny electorates that were used by patrons in order to gain influence in the House of Commons – sometimes sent two MPs to Westminster. Dunwich in Suffolk, with a population of just 32, was one example of such a phenomenon. Agitation for reform grew after the French Revolution and governments, afraid of revolution in Britain, began to extend the franchise with a series of Reform Acts – in 1832, 1867 and 1884. The last of these enfranchised all male house owners in both rural and urban areas, adding six million to the registers of voters. Of course, it would still be some time before women would gain the vote but at least this progress was achieved without the revolutionary activity that took place across Europe several times during the Victorian era.

Life for everyone changed dramatically in Victorian times. Until the 1830s, transport on land had generally been by horse-power or simply walking. The coming of the railways changed everything. Now people who had previously left their immediate environment only rarely, could travel to the coast or to beauty spots or to visit friends. They might have an uncomfortable, and sometimes downright dangerous journey if they travelled third class, but unprecedented opportunities now opened up for them. And goods could be taken from one end of the country to the other quickly. Newspapers began to be truly national as they, too, could benefit from rail transport. This affected politics as politicians were able to get their message around the country via the press or they could travel more easily to different parts of Britain to spread their message. Steam also powered ships crossing the Atlantic and the Channel, as well as the machines that helped to make Britain the 'workshop of the world'.

Living conditions also improved throughout the 63 years of Victoria's reign, as legislation dealt with squalid housing conditions and slum landlords. These did not altogether disappear but the introduction of running water and internal drainage systems in all new residential buildings, as stipulated in the 1875 Public Health Act, undoubtedly improved living conditions and prevented the spread of disease. Working life, too, saw improvements, through a series of Factory Acts that limited the hours worked by women and children and, even, in 1847 gave all factory workers a half-day off on Saturdays. Naturally, unscrupulous employers always found ways to circumvent the new regulations, but they were certainly steps in the right direction.

There is no escaping the fact that to be poor in Victorian times was harsh, whether it was in 1837 when the new young monarch had just come to the throne or at the end of the century when she was becoming old and frail. The only way to get the wherewithal to live, albeit frugally, was to enter the harsh world of the workhouse. Grinding poverty remained a blight on the country that considered itself the most industrially advanced in the world. And power lay throughout the period in the hands of an elite: a wealthy, aristocratic, landowning class that had little knowledge of the way most people lived. The maintenance of the Corn Laws in order to fill the pockets of those who already had plenty, to the cost of those who had very little, was little short of shameful and they were only repealed with great difficulty and the determination of the Prime Minister at the time, Sir Robert Peel.

The Victorian era was one of extremes – grinding poverty and extraordinary wealth, exploitation and generous charity, and innovation and unyielding conservatism. Perhaps that helps to explain the fascination of the period for the reader interested in discovering a past that greatly informs our present.

1

The 1830s:
Reform, Unrest and a New Queen

Whigs and Tories

During the 1830s four men occupied the office of Prime Minister – the Duke of Wellington (1769-1852), Earl Grey (1764-1845), Viscount Melbourne (1779-1848) and Sir Robert Peel (1788-1850). Melbourne and Wellington would, in fact, go on to twice occupy the highest office in the land. It was a decade marked by important reforms and great unrest, giving these four eminent politicians much with which to contend. A great deal of the trouble was caused by the agitation for parliamentary reform that had been stirred up by the political issues of the last two years of the previous decade.

In February 1828, following a campaign by Protestant dissenters, Lord John Russell (1792-1878), the leader of the Whig opposition in the House of Commons, brought forward a bill to repeal the Test and Corporation Acts. The Test Act and the Corporation Act of 1661 had the purpose of restricting Roman Catholics and Nonconformists – Protestants who refused to conform to the strictures of the established Church of England – from holding public office. Although these measures were engrained in Tory sensibilities, Russell's bill passed in the Commons by 44 votes and also flew through the House of Lords. In effect, little changed for Nonconformists because these statutes had not been enforced for some considerable time. However, it represented the thin end of the wedge for many, especially regarding Catholic emancipation which was seen as a tangible erosion of the legal and religious basis on which the establishment stood. But both Wellington, the Tory Prime Minister and the Home Secretary, Sir Robert Peel, although publicly espousing the maintenance of the status quo for many years, began to support reform in private, Peel admitting that 'though emancipation was a great danger, civil strife was a greater danger'. They believed the Union between Great Britain and Ireland of 1800 to be at risk if emancipation stalled. Their actions, however, were viewed as treacherous by those Tory MPs and peers, known as 'Ultras', who believed that the Tory Party's main purpose was to uphold the Church of England. This inevitably led to political turmoil.

There were mass demonstrations in Ireland in support of Catholic emancipation and Wellington managed to persuade a reluctant King George IV (r. 1820-30) that there was no alternative to reform. In February, Wellington and Peel announced their support for emancipation but by this time it looked as if they had done no more than concede to extremists in Ireland. And the Irish were not altogether happy. Many of them disliked the measure because Catholics were still excluded from a number of senior government posts. To make matters worse, the New Catholic Association, founded by the Irish political leader, Daniel O'Connell (1775-1847), was banned, together with a number of other Irish political organisations. Furthermore, the number of Irish who could vote was also reduced.

With Wellington's government in crisis, another serious issue re-emerged – that of parliamentary reform. The Ultras, once vehemently opposed to reform, now embraced it, judging that, because Catholic emancipation was so unpopular with the mainly Protestant British people, a more representative House of Commons would never have passed the 1829 Roman Catholic Relief Act. Liberal Tories, equally disgruntled at their leaders and the opposition party, the Whigs, saw that reform was becoming popular in the country, and, therefore, supported it. Organisations, known as political unions, that championed reform, began to spring up in England's main cities. They consisted of a wide range of opinion and background, from Tory bankers to radical activists from the working class. Against this background, in February 1830, opposition MP, Lord John

Russell, proposed that parliamentary seats be transferred to the great cities of Leeds, Manchester and Birmingham to widen parliamentary representation.

These were difficult times. The banking crisis known as the Panic of 1825 had resulted in the closure of six London banks and sixty country banks in England and there was still a shadow over the country's economy. In the following years, food prices escalated, the crisis amplified by a series of bad harvests. Meanwhile, unemployment rose, leading to strikes in the north of England. Agricultural workers in the south and east of the country participated in the 'Swing Riots', destroying farm machinery in response to increasing mechanisation. Then, in the midst of this turmoil, George IV died. At that time, the death of a monarch meant the dissolution of Parliament and a general election. The incumbent, Wellington, fared badly, losing 178 seats while the Ultras gained 60. Wellington remained resolutely against reform, however, stating in Parliament in November in an answer to a question by Earl Grey that:

'Britain possessed a Legislature which answered all the good purposes of legislation, and this to a greater degree than any legislature ever had answered in any country whatever.'

In other words, he was perfectly happy with things the way they were and, after his U-turn on Catholic emancipation, he wanted it to be known that he was sticking to his principles on parliamentary reform. Those principles, however, brought a vote of no confidence on 15 November and the Whigs, who had been in opposition for all but a couple of years since 1774, returned to power under Earl Grey.

The Reform Act of 1832

Parliamentary reform was the burning issue of the day, but Earl Grey was not entirely supportive. As he himself told the House of Lords in November 1831, 'There is no one more decided against annual parliaments, universal suffrage and the ballot, than I am.' He and his cabinet had one objective – to put a halt to thoughts of extensive reform. Nonetheless, to the dismay of the new king, William IV (r. 1830-37), Grey was insistent on introducing *some* parliamentary reform and on 1 March 1831, with the country, as the Duke of Wellington put it, 'in a state of insanity about reform', Lord John Russell introduced the government's reform bill. It seemed that Grey and his cabinet colleagues had gone with the prevailing wind and the bill was slightly more radical than might have been expected. The counties were given increased representation and eleven of the country's larger towns were each allocated two Members of Parliament. Before this, MPs customarily represented boroughs, the electorates of which numbered anywhere between a dozen and 12,000. Sixty 'rotten boroughs', constituencies with very small electorates that were controlled by a patron to gain influence in the House of Commons, were to be completely disenfranchised. The bill limped through a second reading in Parliament, passing by one vote only. As it began to look as if it was going to be defeated, Grey persuaded the king to dissolve Parliament and call an election, less than 12 months after the last one.

The election which took place between April and June 1831, was, of course, dominated by the bill and it was evident that the general public was clamouring for its passing. Grey won by a landslide and, on returning to Parliament, Lord John Russell immediately introduced a second reform bill. It passed its second reading in the Commons a month after the election by 136 votes but the Tories then attempted to delay it in committee. Nonetheless, it made it through a third reading in September and proceeded to the House of Lords. In October, however, the Lords rejected it by 41 votes. News of this produced an outbreak of violence around the country. In London, the windows of the houses of the ruling elite were smashed; in Nottingham, the residence of the Duke of Newcastle was burned to the ground by a mob; and in Bristol, the bishop's palace and other buildings were attacked. It took three days to restore order in the latter city, and the army finally had to be sent in. Frightened politicians were mindful of what had happened in France in the last decade of the eighteenth century and compromises began to be discussed. Grey even came to an accommodation with the king that, if the Lords once again blocked the bill, sufficient new peers would be created to see it through Parliament.

A third, slightly amended Reform Bill was now introduced in the Commons. It contained some compromises and finally passed its third reading in March 1832. In the Lords, Grey managed to get the bill through its second reading, persuading some of the bishops to change their minds and also cajoling some Tory peers to vote in favour of it. The government lost a vote a few weeks later following a resolution by Wellington's former Lord Chancellor, Lord Lyndhurst, regarding the disenfranchisement of the rotten boroughs and, when the king reneged on his promise to create peers who would see it through the upper house, Grey's government was left with no option other than to resign. The Duke of Wellington eagerly accepted the king's request that he try to form a government, but much of the country was aghast at the idea of Wellington returning to power. There was a run on the Bank of England, deepening the economic crisis further. The Radical leader and social reformer, Francis Place, devised the slogan 'To stop the Duke, go for gold' in order to encourage opposition to Wellington. It was unnecessary, however, as Wellington failed in his efforts to form a government. The king was forced to turn once more to Grey and again promised to provide sufficient peers to see the Reform Bill through Parliament. Wellington, realising that reform of some kind was inevitable, instructed his party in the Lords to abstain and on 4 June 1832, the bill finally passed by 106 votes to 22. Similar measures for Scotland and Ireland followed soon after. For Earl Grey this represented an extraordinary victory which he exploited by calling another general election in which he increased his party's majority.

Grey's reform was just about as much as the establishment could stomach as well as being the least that would be acceptable to ordinary people looking for greater equality in government. But it did stave off the possibility of revolution and social unrest and, as such, it was very welcome. It had the effect of enfranchising the property-owning middle class and the Whigs hoped that this was the new normal – the Whigs at the top of the landed interest, supported by the middle class. But, although the Whigs won many rural seats in the election, the landed interest was divided, in the long run, between Tories and Whigs and in years to come, the Tories who had voted Whig returned to their original leanings, voting Tory once more.

The Reform Act – the Representation of the People Act of 1832, as it was formally known – disenfranchised 56 rotten boroughs that contained less than 2,000 people. One of the MPs was removed from each of 30 boroughs that had fewer than 4,000 inhabitants. There was an increase in county seats from 92 to 159. Larger conurbations such as Manchester, Leeds, Birmingham, Bradford and Sheffield were allocated two MPs each and smaller towns such as Rochdale and Salford, were each allocated one MP. Forty-shilling freeholders held on to the right to vote, but the franchise was extended to owners and long-term leaseholders of land that was worth £10. Medium-term leaseholders on land worth £50 also gained the vote as well as tenants who paid that sum in annual rent. In Scotland, Glasgow was allocated two MPs and county constituencies were introduced. Ireland was given five new MPs representing boroughs. The electorate in England and Wales increased from 350,000 to 650,000; in Scotland it grew from a paltry 5,000 to 65,000; but in Ireland it increased only slightly, from 75,000 to 90,000. In England and Wales, one in seven adult males now had the vote, one in eight in Scotland and a disappointing one in twenty in Ireland.

It is worth noting that despite these apparently radical changes, Grey and his Whig government had achieved what they set out to do, maintaining the position of the landed interest, and many of the constituencies still remained in the grasp of powerful landowners. The system, moreover, remained biased towards England, despite the redistribution of seats. Annual parliaments, universal suffrage and the ballot had all gone by the board. Nonetheless, the will of the people, expressed through protest, riots, campaigns and petitions, had been listened to. Although disappointing to many who had campaigned for it, the act did the trick. Soon after its passing, the economy began to pick up and the threat of unrest in Britain seemed to have passed, for the moment.

Consequences of the Reform Act of 1832

While Britain appeared to have avoided political unrest, many parts of Europe were undergoing disorder and revolution. The July 1830 Revolution in France led to the overthrow of the Bourbon King, Charles X (r. 1824-30) and his replacement by Louis-Philippe, Duke of Orléans (r. 1830-48). In Belgium, revolution focused on independence erupted in Brussels in August 1830, followed by uprisings in other parts of the country. Independence from the Netherlands was declared in October after heavy fighting and the London Conference of major powers of 1830 recognised Belgium's independence and neutrality. Revolutions also took place in Poland and Switzerland. In Italy, insurrection was crushed by the Austrian army and many radicals were arrested. Thus, the achievement of Great Britain, in increasing the franchise, introducing reform and maintaining stability, was admired across a Europe in turmoil.

The Reform Act changed British politics forever. The

relationship of government, Parliament, the electorate and the public was irredeemably altered. Without the corrupt influence of the rotten boroughs and their powerful patrons, the House of Commons gained a new impetus and independence. MPs now paid less attention to the government of the day and instead listened more to the electorate and the general public. Constituency issues took on a new importance and public opinion now had to be listened to. The consequences of ignoring it could be seen in events across the Channel. The old patrician, authoritarian government style was a thing of the past and single constituency issues could bring down a government.

With the electorate now so powerful that it could unseat a government – something that could not happen prior to 1830 – the two main political parties were forced to introduce a concerted national approach to general elections. The Carlton Club was opened for Tories and the Reform Club for Whigs. These two clubs became the centres for distributing party funds, welcoming party workers from the provinces and managing their election campaigns.

Most importantly, the new political landscape gave British people the hope that many of the pressing issues of the day – issues for too long ignored by the Tories – would be dealt with.

The Whig Decade

Having been out of power for so many of the previous 58 years, the Whigs would now remain in government until 1841. It would be a period of reform and change, the necessary parliamentary reform having been the first step. The Whigs now attempted to prove their liberal, progressive credentials by turning to the social, economic, political and religious issues that were foremost in the minds of the British people. The party certainly had the talent to achieve much. The cabinet included one former Prime Minister, Lord Goderich (1782-1859), but there were no fewer than four men in it who would also one day occupy that office – Lord Melbourne, Lord John Russell, Lord Palmerston (1784-1865) and Lord Stanley (1799-1869). They were undoubtedly talented, but it proved difficult to manage such a group of egos. Nonetheless, much was done through the more focused, professional approach to politics. Parliamentary sessions were lengthened in order to cram in as much as possible. Britain moved from the type of state over which Wellington had presided – a state that seemed to exist only to raise finances in order to go to war – to a state that dealt with contemporary issues, issues that affected everyone.

One of the most pressing of these was child labour. Amazingly, it had never been much considered until the notions of workers' rights, children's rights and universal schooling began to be discussed. In 1788, for instance, around two-thirds of the people working in water-powered textiles factories were children. In 1784, a serious outbreak of fever in Manchester cotton mills instigated debate about the conditions in which children worked and the Health and Morals of Apprentices Act – often known as the Factories Act – the first important piece of labour legislation, was passed in 1802. This act took small steps towards protecting children in employment, limiting working hours to 12 per day and abolishing night work for children. It required that employers provided basic education and sleeping accommodation and clothing. The act was not enforced effectively and only applied to apprentices, failing to take into consideration children employed independently – 'free children' – and there were soon many more of these than apprentices. As industrialisation continued at a pace, the number of working children escalated rapidly and there was a great deal of public concern at the conditions under which they were employed. The efforts of the industrialist and philanthropic social reformer Robert Owen (1771-1858) led to the Cotton Mills and Factories Act of 1819 which limited to twelve the number of hours a child could work and prohibited children under the age of nine from being employed.

Two Tories took up the cause of child labour – the MP for Aldborough, Michael Sadler (1780-1835), and Lord Ashley (1801-85) who would later become the Earl of Shaftesbury. The social reformer, Edwin Chadwick (1800-90), a follower of the English philosopher and social reformer, Jeremy Bentham (1748-1832), also played a part in the drafting of the bill and would be hugely influential in public health and social reform for the ensuing two decades. These men succeeded in creating a parliamentary committee on child labour in the textile industry which led to the groundbreaking Factory Act of 1833. Despite the opposition of manufacturers and laissez-faire capitalists, the bill passed through Parliament. It covered almost all textile factories and limited the working week for children aged between nine and thirteen to forty-eight hours; they had to attend school for at least two hours a day; and, most importantly, an inspectorate was instituted to police the new regulations.

The Whig approach to Ireland was far more conciliatory than that of the previous administration which had used coercion and treated the Irish as backward and hostile. They reasoned that the Irish were British citizens and should be treated as such. Whether Irish political leaders such as Daniel O'Connell would accept this was another matter entirely. The failure of Catholic emancipation had persuaded them already that the British government did not really have the best interests of the Irish as part of the Union at heart. O'Connell and his followers – with the support of Irish priests – persevered with their efforts to have the 1800 Act of Union repealed. The 1832 election returned 42 Irish Repeal MPs to Westminster, providing O'Connell with substantial support. In 1833, as discontent escalated, the Whig government responded with yet another bill to use force to deal with disorder in Ireland – the Local Disturbances, etc. (Ireland) Act. This, the latest in a series of what were called Coercion Acts, provided the Lord Lieutenant of Ireland – Marquess Wellesley (1760-1842) – with a number of extra powers, such as the authority to declare curfews and ban meetings deemed subversive. It was never really used, however.

The Irish Church Temporalities Act was a more conciliatory gesture. It aimed to introduce changes to the Church of Ireland, the Church for the minority Irish Protestants in Ireland, in order to render it less objectionable to the majority Catholics. Two archbishoprics and eighteen bishoprics were abolished. This meant that Irish ratepayers no longer had to pay as much to maintain what they perceived as an alien Church. None of the money saved, however, was redirected to the Irish Catholic Church, to the dismay of O'Connell and his supporters. Needless to say, the act did not please Tories either who viewed it as an assault on the Anglican Church. The bill was passed but it led to a number of resignations from Grey's cabinet. The departure of one – Chancellor of the Exchequer, Lord Althorp (1782-1845) – led to the resignation of Grey himself.

Lord Melbourne replaced him as Prime Minister,

immediately turning his attention to the Poor Law. Poverty had escalated in the sixteenth century with the rapid increase in the population. This was exacerbated by Henry VIII's dissolution of the monasteries, which removed rich religious institutions that provided a measure of poor relief. In 1552, the Poor Act placed responsibility for dealing with poverty on parishes which raised money through voluntary contributions. Towards the end of the sixteenth century, authorities began to focus on the deservedly needy – orphans, the elderly and those with mental or physical disabilities and, in 1601, the Elizabethan Poor Law was passed which remained unaltered until 1834, making each parish responsible for the support of the needy in their area. Wealthier citizens were taxed in order to fund basic shelter, clothing and food. By the early 1830s, spending on the Poor Law had rocketed, hitting £7 million. A Royal Commission declared that too much was being spent on poor relief and that the system was unwieldy. In 1834, therefore, the Poor Law Amendment Act was drafted, incorporating the thinking of the Commission. The most important point it made was that people who were unwilling to work should not be so generously subsidised. Sometimes they were found to be better off than those in gainful employment. The workhouse now became the vehicle by which the poor were helped and conditions in workhouses would be deliberately made as harsh as possible, so that they became a place of last resort for the poor. But they were now the only means of obtaining relief. Elected Poor Law guardians would oversee them and it was in their interests to keep costs as low as possible so that they would be ensured of re-election. In financial terms, the Poor Law was very successful, the government spending £4 million less on the poor of England and Wales every year by 1837. It was different for the poor, of course, for whom workhouses were a disaster. They were little more than prisons, but remained operative in one way or another until 1948 when the last vestiges of the Poor Law disappeared, as did the workhouses.

An undercurrent of concern about Ireland and the possibility that Melbourne might take further steps against the established Church there led to him being dismissed by a worried King William. The monarch's choice to take his place was the Tory Sir Robert Peel but, because the Whigs still held a majority in the Commons, Peel was forced to form a minority government. Peel would be the last Prime Minister to be appointed by the British monarch against the wishes of the majority of Members of Parliament. Almost immediately, at Peel's request, the king dissolved Parliament and an election was declared.

The 1835 general election is famous for Peel's 'Tamworth Manifesto', issued the year before in the town of that name. In his manifesto, generally acknowledged as the basis for the modern British Conservative Party, Peel stated that the Conservatives would accept the changes of the 1832 Reform Act, describing it as 'a final and irrevocable settlement of a great constitutional question'. Thus, he signalled a more moderate approach and distanced his party from the views of the Ultra Tories. He promised a review of civil and ecclesiastical institutions and that his government would deal with abuses in the system. It would also examine the issue of church reform in order to ensure the preservation of the 'true interests of the established religion'. Whilst assuring the electorate that the Conservative Party would reform so that it had a future, he was also against change for change's sake. He would, he said, try to avoid 'a fearful vortex of agitation'.

In the election which took place between 6 January and 6 February 1834, the Tories gained 98 seats but the Whigs easily retained their overwhelming majority in the Commons. The situation was untenable and Peel was inevitably forced to resign just three months after the election, a significant defeat for the king whose attempt to install a government against the will of the electorate and sitting MPs had failed so badly and so publicly.

Local government was the next facet of British life to which the Whigs turned their attention. The Municipal Corporations Act, passed through the House at the end of 1835, was the most important and comprehensive piece of local government reform of the nineteenth century. Again, it was the consequence of a Royal Commission that was set up in 1833 with the objective of looking at the ancient closed corporations that were controlling the boroughs.

Hansard reported on 14 February 1833 that its brief was:

> '…to inquire into the state of the Municipal Corporations in England, Wales, and Ireland; and to report if any, and what abuses existed in them, and what measures, in their opinion, it would be most expedient to adopt, with a view to the correction of those abuses.'

Prior to this act, power in the boroughs had been concentrated in the hands of a few people who were self-appointed and often Tory. The aim was more democracy and also to allow the large industrial towns that had just recently gained parliamentary representation to establish their own local government authorities. The act made all boroughs, apart from the City of London, uniform in the way they were managed. Each was to have a mayor, aldermen and councillors who would make up the town council. The councillors would be elected by male ratepayers and would remain in office for three years while aldermen would hold office for six years. Mayors would serve a term of just one year. Countless abuses and anomalies were also expunged. The Tories were not at all happy with the bill but could not stop it becoming law in September 1835. It would prove to be one of the most significant reforms of this reforming century. It gave the new corporations the power to levy rates which provided funding for the many urgent projects that had to be completed – better, cleaner supply of water, paving, lighting and road-building, to name but a few. The act also stipulated that each borough must create a police force which would be under the authority of the Home Office.

In the midst of this welter of change and reform, disaster struck close to home. On 16 October 1834, a fire broke out at the Palace of Westminster. Both Houses of Parliament were destroyed as well as most of the other buildings that made up the complex. Only the efforts of firefighters and a change of wind direction saved the eleventh-century Westminster Hall. The Jewel Tower, the Undercroft Chapel and Chapter House of St Stephen's also survived. King William offered Parliament the use of Buckingham Palace, mainly because he hated the place, but it was not suitable for use as a Parliament. While debate proceeded as to how the building could be replaced, the White Chamber and the Painted Chamber in the old palace were quickly renovated and the politicians moved into those areas. Eventually, it was decided to hold a competition in order to find the best new design for the building. In 1836, the plan of the architect Charles Barry (1795-1860), for a neo-Gothic palace, was declared the winner. Fellow architect Augustus Pugin (1812-52) was drafted in to help in the project because of his leading role in the Gothic Revival style of architecture. The Lords Chamber was completed in 1847, the Commons Chamber in 1852 and the reconstruction of the palace was finally completed around 1870.

Things had changed radically in Britain. No longer was the government's responsibility simply raising revenue and keeping the nation safe. The Whigs had now begun to intervene in the daily life of people in a way that no previous government had. In 1836, the civil registration of births, marriages and deaths was introduced. Prior to this these tasks had been the responsibility of the local vicar. Naturally, this provided the government with useful statistical information but it also made marriages by anyone who was not an Anglican vicar illegal. Death certificates became mandatory and they now had to contain more information such as the cause of death. This had the unexpected benefit of reducing the number of murders committed in Britain as every death had to be examined by a doctor or medical officer.

Lord John Russell, no stranger to reform, had succeeded Melbourne at the Home Office and he began to make important changes. He introduced inspectors for prisons and, in a series of seven acts passed in 1837, the death penalty was removed as an option from all non-violent crimes apart from treason. Cruel sports such as bear-baiting were banned and no longer could one be punished by being put in the pillory.

A New Queen and a General Election

An increasingly frail King William IV finally died at Windsor Castle in the early hours of the morning of 20 June 1837. He had no legitimate living issue – his ten illegitimate children with his mistress, the actress Dorothea Jordan (1761-1816), known as 'Mrs Jordan' did not count – and the crown, therefore, passed to his niece, the unmarried Princess Victoria of Kent (1819-1901) who was the daughter of Prince Edward, Duke of Kent (1767-1820), fourth son of George III (r. 1760-1820). One complication was that she could not become Elector of Hanover, as British monarchs before her had done, because she was a woman and the law of primogeniture applied in Hanover – only men could ascend the throne. Thus, her uncle, the Duke of Cumberland (1771-1851), last surviving son of George III, became Elector. Once more the change of monarch occasioned a general election in Britain which was won, yet again, by the Whigs, although the Conservatives did gain 41 seats. The Whigs, however, still enjoyed a majority of 30 in the Commons.

The new queen was just 18 when she came to the throne, a naive girl who had no real friends and little knowledge of politics. To help her in the early years of her reign, however, she benefitted by having Lord Melbourne as adviser. He did a good job but probably influenced Her Majesty into becoming something of a Whig in her political views. This would change later, after the 1870s when she turned more

Tory due to her dislike of William Gladstone (1809-98).

In May 1839, Melbourne's government suffered a defeat in the Commons over its handling of a matter in Jamaica. To Victoria's annoyance, Melbourne resigned and she was forced to ask Sir Robert Peel to form a government. She disliked Peel intensely, finding him distant and formal but, he failed to form a minority government. His efforts to do so became mired in one of the most bizarre crises in British political history – the 'Bedchamber Crisis'. This centred on the Ladies of the Bedchamber, the women who looked after the Queen on public occasions and very often became close friends of Her Majesty. They were all customarily the wives of eminent nobles and Peel insisted that the Queen replaced Whig ladies with those whose husbands were Tories. As has been noted, Victoria herself had Whig leanings and she was not about to surround herself with women of the opposite persuasion. Therefore, she refused and there was nothing for Peel to do but to withdraw his efforts to form a government. On 10 May 1839, just three days after his resignation, Melbourne resumed his duties as Prime Minister, a post he would hold until 1841. Thereafter, however, the appointment of Ladies of the Bedchamber became non-political.

Reform continued. The stamp duty on newspapers was reduced from 4d to 1d. This made newspapers cheaper and circulation increased accordingly as they were now affordable to the poor and the middle classes. The price of the *Times*, for instance, fell from 7d in the 1820s to 3d in the 1860s. More national and local newspapers appeared and the expansion of the railway increased distribution, taking newspapers around the country.

In education, too, change was afoot. Amazingly, until the 1820s, there were only two universities in England and Wales – the great institutions of Oxford and Cambridge. Even these were restricted, however. Non-Anglicans were barred from taking a degree. At Cambridge, non-Anglicans were permitted to matriculate and study, but were prohibited from graduating. The teaching at Oxford and Cambridge, too, was restricted, focusing on the Classics, mathematics and theology. Other subjects, including the sciences, were ignored. There were four universities in Scotland, at Edinburgh, Glasgow, Aberdeen and St Andrews and these were generally viewed as more progressive than their English counterparts, providing a more practical and modern curriculum. 1827 brought the first new university college in England and Wales. Oddly, it was located at Lampeter, a fairly remote town in Wales. St David's College was established for the sole purpose of training men for the Anglican clergy in Wales. At the same time, however, there was an impulse, spearheaded by radicals such as George Grote (1794-1871) and Joseph Hume (1777-1855), to found a modern and, importantly, secular, university in London. Consequently, London University opened its doors in 1826 with a mission to teach the arts, law and medicine. Religious affiliation was unimportant and, in fact, divinity was not even on the curriculum. The Anglican King's College, London, followed in 1831. In 1836, London University changed its name to University College, London and the name 'University of London' was coined for the examining body for the two London universities. Another Anglican university was opened at Durham in 1833 but that would be the last higher education establishment until the creation of the first college for women – Bedford College – in London in 1849.

The Rise of Chartism

Political reform was still on the agenda of some MPs, radicals such as George Grote and Joseph Hume. Motions for Parliament to be elected annually and for further expansion of the franchise, were looked upon unfavourably by the Whig government and were rejected by an uninterested House of Commons. Indeed, by 1836, radicals were becoming increasingly disillusioned with the government, despite its record of reform in recent times. Out of such dissatisfaction arose the best-known of Britain's radical political movements after the Reform Act – the Chartist movement.

The movement, which would be most active from 1838 to 1848, derived its name from the People's Charter, a manifesto that demanded six reforms that would make the British political system more democratic. These were:

the vote for every man of 21 years of age who was of sound mind and who was not undergoing punishment for a crime; the secret ballot; the abolition of a property qualification for Members of Parliament; payment of MPs, so that a wider range of people could enter Parliament; the appropriate number of voters for constituencies, doing away with the abuse of smaller, less populated constituencies carrying as much or even more weight than larger ones; and annual parliamentary elections to reduce the risk of bribery and intimidation of voters. The movement is usually acknowledged to have begun following the founding in 1836 of the London Working Men's Association by William Lovett (1800-77), who was born in Cornwall and moved to London to work as a cabinet maker, and Francis Place (1771-1854) who worked as a tailor in Temple Bar in London. Like them, Chartists were, more often than not, drawn from the working classes but their demands were strictly political, not social or economic.

Chartism began as a non-violent movement but soon it had its share of activists who advocated any means in order to bring about the change they demanded, men such as the Irish Protestant barrister and MP, Feargus O'Connor (1796-1855). O'Connor had founded the London Democratic Association in 1837 as a radical rival to the London Working Men's Association. The Leeds newspaper, that he published – the *Northern Star* – became the principal publication of the Chartist movement and in its pages, he agitated for a general strike. Even more radical were another Irish lawyer, Bronterre O'Brien (1805-64) and a man described as 'Chartism's *enfant terrible*', Julian Harney (1817-97), both advocates of revolution in Britain. One man who led a genuine attempt at armed revolution was John Frost (1784-1877), a draper from Newport, Monmouthshire. Fourteen of his followers were killed and Frost and two fellow revolutionaries were sentenced to be hanged, drawn and quartered – the last men to be sentenced to this particular form of capital punishment – but their sentences were commuted by the cabinet to transportation for life.

The Chartist movement began to split into two factions. On the one side were the militant, 'physical force' Chartists, and on the other the 'moral force', moderate Chartists. Nonetheless, huge rallies in 1838 in many of the country's biggest cities and a national convention in London the following year demonstrated the growing desire for more reform in the nation's political system. The convention was controlled by the moderate wing of the movement which wanted to present Parliament with a petition in support of the six demands. If the politicians rejected the petition, however, the Chartists planned to call a general strike. The petition, containing one million signatures, was brought to Parliament in a cart by Thomas Attwood (1783-1856), the MP for Birmingham, but, after being debated, it was roundly rejected by a vote of 235 to 46.

Fearing the intensity of feeling after this rejection and

concerned that there really would be an uprising, the Whig government appointed the former soldier, General Sir Charles Napier (1782-1853) to supervise the north of the country where feeling was running very high. He cleverly invited Chartist leaders to a demonstration of military firepower in order to convince them that, if they chose to lead an insurrection, they would have no chance of success. By 1840, many of them were in prison and, with the economy on the rise, the agitation died down. It would return, however.

There was a great deal of political change around this time, but while the politicians were arguing in Westminster, there were other huge changes in the rest of the country and abroad in Britain's colonial possessions. It is astonishing to think that there were just 338 miles of railway track in the country in 1835. Within the next six years this increased to 1,775 miles. Meanwhile, industry was also changing. The amount of raw cotton used in Britain increased from 318 million pounds in 1835 to 459 million pounds in 1840, and cotton factory workers increased in number from 220,000 to 264,000 in the same period.

Innovations of the 1830s

The nineteenth century brought dramatic changes to people's everyday lives. Technology, in particular the development of machines, was behind most of them. For the first time in human history, people did not have to rely on animal, human or natural power. Steam now became the force that powered machines and provided new means of transport at what were, for the time, incredible speeds. Work and leisure would never be the same again.

In the beginning, steam engines were stationary machines that pumped water out of mines or made factory machines work. By the end of the reign of George III, however, steam was being used to propel vehicles, especially boats. A Scotsman, William Symington (1764-1831) patented a marine steam engine and, in 1802, his steamship, the *Charlotte Dundas*, towed two 70-ton boats for 19 miles along the Forth and Clyde Canal. The American, Robert Fulton (1765-1815) began running a steamboat passenger service on the Hudson in 1807. After 1815, steamboat services were established connecting Liverpool and Glasgow, and Holyhead and Dublin. The first cross-Channel steamboat service was launched in 1818 and the Atlantic Ocean was crossed for the first time by a ship with steam engines in 1819 when the *Savannah* reached New York. It should be noted, however, that the majority of the crossing was conducted under sail. The Canadian ship, the *Royal William*, made the first crossing entirely using steam power in 1833. It took her 21 days to get from Pictou, Nova Scotia, to London. Not long after, the great British engineer, Isambard Kingdom Brunel's (1806-59) steamship, the *Great Western*, crossed the Atlantic from Bristol to New York in 13 days, launching a regular service that lasted until 1846. Screw propellers were being fitted around this time but sail power was still used for transporting goods, and tea clippers set record times between Britain and the Far East in the middle of the nineteenth century. Their advantage lay in not being weighed down by the many tons of coal that steamships had to carry to fuel the engines. It would not be until the opening of the Suez Canal that sailing ships would lose their competitive edge and soon the great shipping lines would be created – Cunard, P&O and White Star, for instance – taking passengers and mail around the globe.

The railway developed alongside easier ocean travel. The Cornish engineer, Richard Trevithick (1771-1833) built one of the earliest steam-powered locomotives in 1804, his engine transporting a carriage of passengers by road. A little later, George Stephenson (1781-1848) built an engine for transporting coal six miles from a colliery to the River Tyne. In 1814, his engine *Blücher*, named for the great Prussian general, was pulling thirty tons of coal up a hill, reaching the dizzying speed of four miles an hour. It was Stephenson who conceived of a carriage pulled by an engine running on rails. Appointed engineer on the first two railway lines to be built – the Stockton and Darlington of 1825 and the Liverpool and Manchester of 1830 – he built the *Rocket* in 1829 which won the Rainhill Trials, a competition staged by the directors of the Liverpool and Manchester Railway to decide whether stationary steam engines or locomotives should be used to pull the trains on their tracks. When the railway opened the following year, *Rocket* achieved a speed of 30 miles per hour. It was not to everyone's taste, however. The MP Thomas Creevey (1768-1838) famously said of it:

'This infernal nuisance – the locomotive Monster, carrying eighty tons of goods, and navigated by a tail of smoke and sulphur, coming through every man's grounds between Manchester and Liverpool.'

Five further railway lines opened under the control of George Stephenson, and his son Robert (1803-59), who also designed the Menai Strait Railway Bridge and was responsible for the building of the London and Birmingham Railway which opened in 1838. Joining up with other, older railway lines, it became the London and North-Western Railway in 1846. Another great railway engineer was Isambard Kingdom Brunel, who, as we have seen, also built steamships. He designed and built the railway line from Paddington to Bristol – the Great Western Railway – between 1838 and 1841 and designed the magnificent Clifton Suspension Bridge. The competition for railways was provided by canals which provided a cheap means of transportation of coal and other heavy goods. Canal travel was slow, however, and gradually began to be overtaken by rail transport, as did stage coaches.

The conditions in which rail passengers were carried sometimes left a great deal to be desired. First class passengers, of course, had some comfort, their carriages being covered and possessing glass windows. Second class passengers also enjoyed some of these comforts, but third class was uncomfortable and could even be described as dangerous. They were charged only a penny per mile but often there were no seats and sometimes their carriages did not even have sides. The satirical magazine *Punch* had some fun with their discomfort in a piece entitled 'Rules for the Railways':

'No Third Class carriage is to contain more than a foot of water in wet weather; but, to prevent accidents, corks and swimming belts should always be kept in open carriages.'

Railways were often very local and run by small companies but through time these were amalgamated to create the seven or eight large companies that would last into the next century. However, even the small companies before amalgamation were large businesses and, by 1853, they each employed more than 2,500 people. A lot of money was needed to build a railway and the principle of the joint-stock company was employed, shares being sold to the general public to raise funds. These shareholdings were organised in such a way that investors could not lose more than they put in. Before long, the shares in railway companies were available to be bought and sold on the stock exchange. This was an important development in finance. Before this time, the stock exchange dealt mainly in government funds and the railways, therefore, can be said to have helped to develop the way we now do business and invest. Of course, those who invested hoped that their investment would appreciate in time but this got out of hand in what is known as the 'railway mania' of 1845 to 1847, when people gambled recklessly with railway shares. The crash that inevitably followed was disastrous for many.

Another important benefit derived from the development of the railway was that Greenwich Mean Time became the standard for time throughout Great Britain. Previously, time was a local matter, judged by the position of the sun in the sky. The introduction of standard railway timetables, such as George Bradshaw's *Monthly Railway Guide*, first published in 1841, necessitated the standardisation of time throughout the country. The economic benefits of the railways were many. Salesmen could travel more widely and cover more ground more quickly. The subsequent orders could then be delivered more rapidly. Fresh foods could be delivered to cities that were a distance away from the area in which they were produced, opening up lucrative markets for farmers. National newspapers could be read in all parts of the land for the first time and this had a consequential effect on people's knowledge of and understanding of politics. Politicians were also able to take their message across the country. In the event of unrest and protest, the railway could be used to transport troops around the country quickly. Leisure was opened up and seaside resorts boomed that were accessible by rail. Towns were also created by the railways. Crewe was a village of just 70 residents in 1831, but after the Grand Junction Railway company chose Crewe as the site for its locomotion works and railway station in the late 1830s, it grew in size, having 40,000 inhabitants by 1871. Similarly, Swindon grew inexorably after the Great Western Railway built its repair works there in 1842.

Work, too, was transformed. Affluent employees could afford to live far from their place of work and commute every day. This had the effect of segregating the classes according to where they lived. The working and lower middle-class employees lived near the centres of towns and cities. The middle class lived slightly further out but could afford the fares of the horse-drawn buses. Only those who were better off could afford the train fare and lived often in villages that were strung along a train line. Suburbia came into being.

Charles Darwin

Born in Shrewsbury in 1809, Charles Darwin (1809-82) was the fifth of the six children of a wealthy society doctor and businessman, Robert Darwin (1766-1848). His mother, Susannah (1765-1817) was related to Josiah Wedgwood (1730-95) who founded the famous Wedgwood pottery company. From an early age, Charles was fascinated by natural history. He attended the University of Edinburgh Medical School in 1825 but remained more interested in natural history, learning taxidermy and working on a project looking at the anatomy and life cycle of marine invertebrates in the Firth of Forth. He was a member of the Plinian Society at the university, a radical group that challenged the accepted religious view of science. Having neglected his medical studies, he was sent by his father to Christ's College, Cambridge to study for a BA that would help him to become an Anglican country parson. Once again, however, his love for natural history diverted him from his studies, although he managed to do fairly well in his finals.

In August 1831, he was invited by a Cambridge professor of botany, John Stevens Henslow (1796-1861) to travel as a naturalist – self-funded – on what was planned to be a two-year voyage on HMS *Beagle*. The ship's mission was to chart the coastline of South America. Robert Darwin was not in favour of Charles embarking on such a voyage, regarding it as a waste of time, but was eventually persuaded and his son left on the *Beagle* on 27 December 1831. Instead of the intended two years, the voyage actually lasted five, during which Darwin would spend a great deal of his time on land, collecting specimens and looking at the geology of where he was. The *Beagle* visited Brazil, Patagonia, Tierra del Fuego, Chile, the Galapagos Islands, Australia, South Africa and many other places where Darwin made his observations and collected samples.

He was already something of a celebrity in the scientific world when the *Beagle* eventually returned to Falmouth in Cornwall on 2 October 1836. His father provided the funds for him to pursue his research and many different institutions were working on his finds. By March 1837, he was starting to sketch out his theory of natural selection. In June 1838, he fell ill with health problems that remained with him for the remainder of his life, especially during stressful periods.

After many years of research and writing, his book, *On the Origin of Species*, was published on 22 November 1859, its entire print run of 1,250 copies selling out almost immediately. In the introduction, he succinctly lays out his theory:

'As many more individuals of each species are born than can possibly survive; and as, consequently, there is a frequently recurring struggle for existence, it follows that any being, if it vary however slightly in any manner profitable to itself, under the complex and sometimes varying conditions of life, will have a better chance of surviving, and thus be *naturally selected*. From the strong principle of inheritance, any selected variety will tend to propagate its new and modified form.'

In the book, Darwin does not go into the issue of human origins, although there were hints as to what he believed. Some in the Church of England were favourable, accepting natural selection as just another facet of God's work. The writer Charles Kingsley (1819-75), for instance, a friend and correspondent of Darwin, described it as 'just as noble a conception of Deity'. There was a famous debate at Oxford in 1860 where the Bishop of Oxford, Samuel Wilberforce (1805-73) argued against natural selection and the fact that humans could be descended from apes. Arguing for Darwin's viewpoint was botanist and explorer Joseph Hooker (1817-1911). Meanwhile, when Wilberforce asked the English biologist, Thomas Huxley (1825-95), whether he was descended from apes on his mother's or father's side, Huxley famously replied that he would rather be descended from an ape than a man who misused his great talents to suppress debate.

Translated into many languages, the *Origin of Species* soon became an essential scientific text that elicited interest from all walks of life. Indeed, many working men, curious about the theory, attended lectures given by Huxley on the subject. It became a significant fixture of Victorian culture, being satirised by cartoonists and writers and popularising his theory. Before long, despite others having ideas along the same lines, evolutionism was identified solely with Charles Darwin.

Literature in the 1830s

Journalist, political reformer and agriculturist, William Cobbett (1763-1835) had been a soldier and during that time had gathered evidence of corruption in the ranks above him. He wrote a 1792 book about the poor treatment and low pay in the army, after which, sensing that he was about to be arrested, he fled to France and then the United States. Returning to England in 1800, he began working as a journalist. He went to prison for treasonous libel from 1810 to 1812. In 1817, once again fearing arrest for his anti-government writings, he returned to America, living there for two years. Returning to England, he resumed his attacks on the government. He became particularly interested in the plight of the rural Englishman and began riding around England on horseback, observing what was happening in the English countryside, seeing it from the perspective of a farmer and a social reformer. *Rural Rides* was published in book form in two volumes in 1830.

One man, of course, dominates the literature of the Victorian age – Charles Dickens (1812-70). His first book – *Sketches by Boz* – was published in 1836, a collection of sketches of London scenes and Londoners. The last part of the book consisted of fictional stories. The book, written under Dickens's pen name 'Boz', was brilliantly illustrated by George Cruikshank (1792-1878) and was published in two volumes. Following the great success of this first book, Dickens was asked to write a series that became *The Posthumous Papers of the Pickwick Club*, more often known simply as *The Pickwick Papers*. Written in nineteen instalments, each costing a shilling and still under the name Boz, the book was immensely successful. A sequence of loosely related adventures, it features Dickens's usual cast of splendid characters, including two of his best loved: Samuel Pickwick, Esquire and Sam Weller. Dickens would publish another two novels in the 1830s. *Oliver Twist* appeared in serial form in 1837 to 1839, the novel appearing in three volumes six months before the completion of the serial. It provides an unromantic view of the underworld in his time and vividly exposes the cruelty shown to orphans in the capital in the mid-nineteenth century. Oliver, an orphan born in a workhouse encounters characters such as the Artful Dodger, Bill Sykes, Mr Bumble and the criminal boss, Fagin, with his constant use of the phrase 'my dear'. *Nicholas Nickleby* followed in serial form in 1838 and 1839. In this novel, Dickens deals with social injustices as Nicholas tries to support his mother and sister after the death of his father.

Another towering figure of nineteenth-century literature

was the poet, Alfred, Lord Tennyson (1809-92), who published the first version of his lyrical ballad, 'The Lady of Shalott' in 1833. Its medieval romanticism and mysterious symbolism provided inspiration for a number of artists, most notably the Pre-Raphaelites. Tennyson was Poet Laureate throughout much of Queen Victoria's reign and remains to this day one of Britain's favourite poets.

Victoria and Albert

The marriage of Queen Victoria to Prince Albert of Saxe-Coburg and Gotha had come about at the urging of her uncle, Leopold (r. 1831-65), King of the Belgians. Leopold, the then Princess Victoria's mother, the Duchess of Kent (1786-1861) and Albert's father, Ernest I (r. 1806-44), Duke of Saxe-Coburg and Gotha – all siblings – worked hand in hand to bring the couple together, but William IV was against any association with the Coburgs. He sought a marriage between Princess Victoria and Prince Alexander of the Netherlands (1818-48), the second son of the Prince of Orange, later William II of the Netherlands (r. 1840-49). It was Albert, however, whom Victoria liked most, describing him as:

'...extremely handsome; his hair is about the same colour as mine; his eyes are large and blue, and he has a beautiful nose and a very sweet mouth with fine teeth; but the charm of his countenance is his expression, which is most delightful.'

In contrast, she found Prince Alexander to be very plain and none of the other princes who were paraded before her came close to Albert, in her opinion. She described her happiness in a grateful letter to her Uncle Leopold, thanking him for:

'...the prospect of *great* happiness you have contributed to give me, in the person of dear Albert... He possesses every quality that could be desired to render me perfectly happy. He is so sensible, so kind, and so good, and so amiable too. He has besides the most pleasing and delightful exterior and appearance you can possibly see.'

She was still only 17 and marriage was not yet an immediate prospect. In 1839, however, Albert returned to the United Kingdom and Victoria proposed to him. The couple married at the Royal Chapel, St James's Palace on 10 February 1840. Albert initially found it difficult and the British public did not really take to him. They viewed him as being from an insignificant state and there was undoubtedly anti-German sentiment at work. Because of that, Parliament was reluctant to allow him to be given a peerage. He was given a smaller annuity than consorts of the past. But he was allowed to be styled 'His Royal Highness' and Victoria gave him the title Prince Consort.

After they had been married for a few years, neither of them was particularly daunted by the strong personalities of the politicians with whom they had to deal. Victoria might have felt out of place with the older, better educated and more worldly-wise politicians but she was candid and stubborn – some would even say wilful – and she was never in awe of them. Albert tried throughout their marriage to deal with her character faults but never quite succeeded. He, on the other hand, viewed a monarch's interaction with her politicians differently. He was possessed of a strong sense of the royal prerogative and envisioned a strong, active monarch rather than one that just turned up for ceremonies and rituals. He was very much against the sovereign holding any particular political allegiances, insisting that the Queen should be involved in affairs of state but without having any specific interest. In fact, he and Victoria very much involved themselves in foreign policy, conducting what was almost their own policy by remaining in close contact with their many European relatives, many of whom were occupants of the thrones of their nations. Albert was vindicated in this by the huge success he made of the Great Exhibition in Hyde Park.

2

The 1840s:
The 'Hungry Decade'

Foreign Affairs

Expansion of the empire provided opportunities for emigration and settlement, easing, it was hoped, the overcrowding that was becoming commonplace at home, as Britain's population increased dramatically.

Around this time, New Zealand became a British possession. The individual responsible for this was Edward Gibbon Wakefield (1796-1862), an interesting but fairly unscrupulous character. Born in London, Wakefield served as a King's Messenger, delivering diplomatic mail across Europe during the last few years of the Napoleonic Wars. In 1826, he was arrested after abducting a wealthy fifteen-year-old heiress with a view to marrying her and was jailed for three years in Newgate prison. While incarcerated, he devised colonisation schemes and on his release became part of a plan to colonise South Australia. Withdrawing from that, he was invited to become a director of the New Zealand Company in March 1839, selling land to colonists at £1 per acre. The first pioneers of the new colony began to arrive in 1840. Generally speaking, although there were wars with the indigenous Maoris later, there was not the terrible bloodshed that usually greeted the arrival of colonists.

In Canada, meanwhile, trouble erupted in 1837 between the English-speaking part in Upper Canada and the French-speaking part in Lower Canada, or French Quebec. The French increasingly took exception to being governed by a British minority, which led to fighting around Toronto and Montreal, with the Americans joining in on the side of the rebels. In May of that year, the Earl of Durham (1792-1840), a radical and son-in-law of Earl Grey, was appointed Governor-General of Canada, with Edward Gibbon Wakefield as an influential adviser. Durham took a lenient approach to the rebels, however, which was frowned upon in London and he was forced to resign in October 1838. But he published a *Report on the Affairs of British North America* in which he stated that:

'While the present state of things is allowed to last, the actual inhabitants of these Provinces have no security for person or property – no enjoyment of what they possess – no stimulus to industry.'

Importantly, he insisted that Lower and Upper Canada should be allowed to unite and govern as one country. Britain, he stated, should only be involved in Canada's foreign affairs, its trade and decisions around land rights. The majority of his suggestions were accepted and put into practice by the government, the Act of Union of 1840 uniting the two parts of the territory under a legislative assembly and an elected assembly in which Upper and Lower Canada enjoyed equal representation. Self-government for Canada was eventually provided with the 1867 British North America Act.

In South Africa, as the British enlarged their territory from 1835 onwards, the Boers, Dutch settlers who had arrived in the mid-seventeenth century, started their famous 'Great Trek', a quest to establish their own territory. Lasting from 1835 to 1837, it consisted of around 10,000 farmers and their families who marched to the north and east of the Orange River. They were constantly engaged in fighting with the Zulus, whose land they were taking, and would lose a war with the British in 1842-43. The Trek established the Boer nationalist credo that remained in place in South Africa until the 1990s.

Peel's Poisoned Chalice

The Tamworth Manifesto that Peel produced in 1835 became ever more significant as the 1830s drew to a close. It recognised that politics were changing, becoming more national in scope and, therefore, that national feeling needed to be taken into account when drawing up legislation. Prime Minister Lord Melbourne was losing the initiative to the opposition which was now becoming better known as the Conservative Party rather than the Tory Party. Sir Robert Peel, leader of the Conservatives, accepted that the national feeling for reform and improvement must be acknowledged and he believed his party was the one to champion such desires. After all, the 1837 election had seen them make substantial gains, although the Whigs remained in government. In the general election of June 1841, Peel's Conservatives secured a majority of 70 seats, winning 367 seats to the Whigs' 271 and the Irish Repeal Party's 20.

Sir Robert Peel was the son of the first cotton millionaire of the Industrial Revolution and it was from him that he inherited his baronetcy. Educated at Harrow and at Christ Church, Oxford, Peel entered Parliament as a Tory in 1809, at the age of just 21, representing the Irish pocket borough of Cashel in County Tipperary. Thirty-two years later he became Prime Minister at a propitious moment. The British economy was in very good shape as a result of its growing manufacturing and trade sectors and, indeed, between 1841 and 1851, Britain's gross national product rose from £452 million to £523 million. In the budget of 1842, the first of the new government, and presented by Peel himself, rather than the Chancellor of the Exchequer, Henry Goulburn (1784-1856), income tax was reintroduced, much to the dismay of the well-off. First introduced to help finance the Napoleonic Wars and then abolished in 1817, it amounted to seven pence in the pound on incomes of more than £150 a year. Peel described it as a short-term measure to help deal with the problems of the public finances. But it was a courageous step and would give him some leeway in cutting the import duties that the Tories had introduced in the 1820s and that the Whigs had prolonged in the 1830s. Eighty-five Conservatives voted against the budget and the Duke of Buckingham (1797-1861), heavily invested in the interests of landowners and farmers, resigned from the cabinet over it.

Unfortunately, the success of the British economy, unequalled anywhere in the world, failed to guarantee a settled, happy nation. Indeed, the 1840s were generally a difficult time for Britons. In Ireland, the potato famine that began in 1845 constituted an unmitigated disaster with millions starving to death or being left with no option but to emigrate. There was also the revival of Chartism to be dealt with as the decade advanced. Anger and agitation about the Corn Laws once again gave the government cause to fear revolution and ultimately, therefore, it could be argued that Peel was given something of a poisoned chalice when he won the election of 1841.

From 1837 to 1843, Britain was lost in a morass of depression and anxiety. Poverty and unemployment were rife, leading many to doubt the benefits of industrialisation and urbanisation. The philosopher Thomas Carlyle (1795-1881) was firm in these views throughout the 1830s and continued expressing his doubts during the ensuing decade. In his 1843 book, *Past and Present*, he railed against free-market capitalism and the ways in which labour had changed with the introduction of machinery. He denounced the exploitation of workers by their employers and the low wages and poverty that resulted. He wrote of the unrest he perceived:

> 'The Condition of England on which many pamphlets are now in preparation, and many thoughts unpublished are going on in every reflective head, is justly regarded as one of the most ominous and withal, one of the strangest, ever seen in this world... So many hundred thousands sit in workhouses: and other hundred thousands have not yet got even workhouses; and in thrifty Scotland itself, in Glasgow or Edinburgh City, in their dark lanes, hidden from all but the eye of God, and of rare Benevolence the minister of God, there are scenes of woe and destitution and desolation, such as, one may hope, the Sun never saw before in the most barbarous regions where men dwelt.'

A growing population was one of the major problems. Between 1841 and 1851, the population of England, Wales and Scotland rose from 18.5 million to 20.8 million.

Thus, no matter how well the economy was doing, there simply was not the means to feed those extra mouths to a decent level. People lived in squalid, unsanitary conditions in which infectious diseases such as cholera, typhus and dysentery flourished. The national average life expectancy was 40, although in Manchester it was just 27. In Liverpool, the life expectancy for those of the professional classes was 35, but for tradesmen it was just 22. Other classes of worker died even earlier. The streets were disgusting and dangerous, patrolled by rats, packs of wild dogs and feral cats and cesspools, dungheaps and filth were everywhere.

1842: The Worst Year of the Nineteenth Century

Such terrible conditions led inevitably to a renewed interest in Chartism. In July 1840, a conference was held in Manchester that led to the establishment of a National Charter Association. A campaign of leafleting, pamphleteering and fundraising was launched, supporting the original six Chartist demands which were still the core of the movement. On his release from prison in 1841, Feargus O'Connor began to assemble another petition that was presented to Parliament in May 1842, a document signed, it was claimed, by more than three million people from all over the country. Once again, the House of Commons rejected it, by 287 votes to 59, consigning the lofty ambitions of Chartism once more to failure.

In addition to the terrible living conditions, between 1837 and 1843 Britain was hit by a series of bad harvests. Manufacturing output fell, as did exports. Another financial crisis in 1839 brought a halt even to the construction of railways and no new railways were built between 1839 and 1843. One observer cites 1842 as the worst year of the entire nineteenth century. Workers in the cotton mills in Lancashire and Cheshire were laid off or worked shorter hours with the concomitant reduction in wages. Factories were failing and the number of families on poor relief escalated dramatically. The government was told that 17,000 people in Paisley in Scotland were:

> '...enduring a gradual starvation with exhausted resources, and manifestly impaired health and strength on the part of the people, and with failing funds on the side of the relief committee.'

By the start of summer 1842, the country was in a parlous state. There were strikes and lock-outs across the north and in Scotland. The unemployed in Yorkshire and Lancashire roamed the towns armed with cudgels, looting shops, skirmishing with police and demanding relief from the grinding poverty they and their families were being forced to endure. The private dwellings of magistrates and clergymen were attacked, as well as public buildings. Edwin Chadwick had published his *Report on the Sanitary Condition of the Labouring Population of Great Britain*, linking the dreadful living conditions, the filthy, unsanitary streets and the dirty water with the wave of crime, disease and immorality that was sweeping across Britain. Meanwhile, the young Friedrich Engels (1820-95), manager of his family's cotton mills in Salford, foresaw a revolution by the people in protest at the exploitation by unscrupulous factory owners. His work, *The Condition of the Working Class in England* was based on what he saw in Manchester's cotton mills. Later, he would go on to help Karl Marx (1818-83) develop Marxism.

Of course, it was not all as black and white as some made out. Britain was a complex society and it was not only the people at the bottom of the heap who were dissatisfied with the direction the country was taking. The Great Reform Act had disappointed many in the business and manufacturing classes who saw that little had changed and that – as had been intended by the creators of the act – the aristocracy and wealthy landowners still wielded most influence in government.

The Corn Laws

The influence of the elite on government was manifested in the Corn Laws, legislation passed in 1815 and modified in 1828. These laws were intended, quite simply, to provide protection for the interests of the landed classes and those involved in agriculture; in other words, those who possessed the greatest influence in the House of Commons as well as in the Lords. The Corn Laws eliminated foreign competition, prohibiting the import of wheat until the price in Britain was so high that there was a danger of famine. That price was 73 shillings a quarter and at that level, wheat could be imported virtually free of charge. When the domestic price fell, however, to 54 shillings or less, a tariff of 20 shillings per quarter was imposed on foreign wheat. The bad harvests of the late 1830s and early 1840s brought Britain close to the edge of famine and the laws began to be perceived as an appalling example of parliamentary abuse, corrupt legislation designed to enrich those who passed the laws. Factory owners and businessmen reasoned that were food prices not kept artificially high, their workers would eat and live better, and their demands for higher wages just to feed their families would be dissipated.

Many who campaigned for the repeal of the Corn Laws also had loftier ambitions. They foresaw Britain's adoption of free trade, her abolition of tariffs as a signal to the rest of the world which would follow suit. The world would then not only enjoy unfettered commerce; it would also be a better, more peaceful place. The obstacle to this, as one pamphleteer put it was '…the bread-taxing oligarchy, unprincipled, unfeeling, rapacious and plundering…'

Peel made efforts to reform the Corn Laws in his budget of 1842, making the 20 shilling tariff applicable when the price reached 50 shillings. This budget also reduced duty on around 700 items. Peel's efforts did not go nearly far enough, however, and an organisation named the Anti-Corn Law League, created in 1839, began to agitate for the complete eradication of tariffs on wheat. Its principal leaders were two Radical MPs, John Bright (1811-89) and Richard Cobden (1804-65). Bright was a Quaker manufacturer from Rochdale, and Cobden was an Anglican manufacturer from Manchester. Both men were unquestionable optimists who believed that free trade would bring peace and prosperity to the world. Their organisation would spearhead one of the greatest mass political movements that Britain has ever seen.

If the Chartist movement was of working-class tendencies, the Anti-Corn Law League spread its influence wider, because manufacturers, often middle class, appreciated the idea that repeal of the law would bring an end to agitation for more wages and the unrest this caused. For the working class, the cost of living would go down and the supply of grain for foodstuffs would not be threatened with interruption.

The League's campaign began around 1843, employing newspapers, an endless supply of pamphlets and leaflets and huge rallies with expert orators making the case for repeal. Peel saw the dangers inherent in this mass movement and, as we have seen, made efforts at change. By 1845, he had been persuaded by the dreadful potato famine that was ravaging Ireland that the laws should be repealed but in Parliament he was faced with a strong pro-Corn Law lobby. The Conservative Party, after all, was filled with the very landowners and aristocrats who stood to lose if the laws were repealed. In response to the growing success of the League, support for the Corn Laws also sprang up, with the founding of societies known as the 'Anti-League' in farming communities. On 4 December 1845, Peel announced in the *Times* that Parliament would be recalled in January 1846 to debate the repeal of the Corn Laws. The following day, however, he resigned as Prime Minister, believing that it would be impossible to implement his policy. The Queen asked Lord John Russell to form a government, but he was unable to do so and Peel returned as Prime Minister on 20 January.

Peel was up against it and the debate of his bill was one of the longest ever devoted to a single issue in Parliament. The all-important vote was taken in February 1846 and the Corn Laws were repealed by a majority of 97. Nonetheless, 242 Tories voted against it, siding with the Protectionist faction led by Lord George Bentinck (1802-48) and future Prime Minister, Benjamin Disraeli (1804-81).

A year later, Peel announced his plan, in the form of the Corn and Customs Bill. Tariffs on a variety of manufactured goods were abolished or reduced. Imports of the majority of foodstuffs were made duty-free. Immediately, American maize was allowed to be imported free of duties, and tariffs on all other grains were to be lowered until 1849, after which date they would be subject to a duty of 1 shilling. But, he also had to find a way to compensate the vested interests and, to this end, he abolished the law that anyone in straitened circumstances had to be returned to their place of birth to be looked after. These were often people who had migrated from the countryside to the towns and cities. Local costs for poor relief were reduced and costs for maintenance of roads, the police and criminal prosecutions would henceforth be borne by the government.

Sadly, Peel's reforms did little to help the starving in Ireland. They had no money to buy grain anyway and the tariff did not really disappear until around 1849 when it was already too late for them. Free trade probably did nothing, either, to maintain the country's pre-eminent position in the world. By the 1870s, Britain was beginning to lag behind the increasingly industrialised United States and Germany in the struggle for primacy and with both those nations protected by high tariffs to encourage domestic production, people began to agitate for a return to tariffs. By the start of the twentieth century, Britain, extremely vulnerable to competition from abroad, was trailing behind its competitors.

The Irish Potato Famine

In common with every other part of the United Kingdom, Ireland had experienced rapid population growth since the last few decades of the eighteenth century. In 1800, its population numbered five million, but an additional two million had been added to that number by 1821. By 1841, it was eight million. Thus, it had increased by more than 60 per cent in around 40 years. Until 1815 Ireland enjoyed a substantial textile industry, but the factories of Scotland and the north of England decimated this with mass production and the lower prices this encouraged. Increasingly, too, with a fall in prices for arable products, Irish farmers moved from food production to the rearing of cattle and sheep. Between 1815 and 1845, more than a million people emigrated from Ireland and it is estimated that at least 30 per cent of those who remained behind relied entirely on the potato which was still grown in large quantities. This reliance on one crop brought great dangers, rendering the Irish vulnerable to crop failure. Potatoes could not be kept in storage for more than a year which meant that a plentiful harvest one year could not be used to compensate for a poor one the following year. Crop failures occurred regularly but between 1845 and 1848, the entire crop was destroyed each year by a blight, the result of a fungus, and no one could find a way to prevent it.

Almost a million people, around 12 per cent of the

population of Ireland, died as a result, and diseases such as dysentery and typhus flourished. Lord John Russell described it as 'a famine of the thirteenth century acting upon a population of the nineteenth'. The immediate impact was obviously devastating but it continued to hover like a black cloud over Ireland for decades to come. Many who survived the famine saw no future in their homeland and left. More than one and a half million had emigrated by 1855. Britain, where there was plentiful employment to be had in railway construction, was an obvious destination, but many sailed off to seek their fortune in the New World, the United States – especially the East Coast – being a favoured destination.

The British government's reaction to the Great Famine was negligible and this created hostility to Britain that would erupt in armed violence in the future. The government helped fund Quaker soup kitchens, but estimated that long-term relief would come through the consolidation and eradication of the tiny plots of land that were commonplace in Ireland. The Encumbered Estates Act, passed in 1849, made possible the purchase of small estates by the owners of outside capital and promoted the sale of the land possessed by the rural poor of Ireland. This, the government callously hoped, would encourage more of the rural poor to emigrate to the United States, moving the problem out of their hands.

Poor and Labour Laws

On the same night that the Corn Laws were repealed, Peel's Irish Coercion Bill was defeated in the Commons and a few days later, he resigned. The Whig, Lord John Russell, son of the sixth Duke of Bedford (1766-1839), became Prime Minister. By this time, Russell was an old hand, having served as an MP for more than 30 years. It had been he, of course, who had seen the Great Reform Act through Parliament. Like Peel, he had converted to favouring the repeal of the Corn Laws and, by doing so, had helped the prime minister in no small measure. He was also a great believer in religious tolerance and believed that Protestant dissenters and Jews should have equal rights which, of course, irritated the Anglican right. Still, his championing of the Reform Act had given him the status of something like a national treasure. Although the son of a duke, he was far from a rich man and, from 1847, he lived in a house near Richmond that was given to him by Queen Victoria for life.

The repeal of the Corn Laws, it was hoped, would bring some respite to the working class and help improve the employment situation by cutting the costs of manufacturers. But extreme poverty and unemployment remained a problem. In 1847, in an effort to improve things, a Factory Act was passed that limited to ten hours a day the time that women and children could work. It also, effectively, gave all factory workers half a day off on Saturdays. There were ways around it, however, and unscrupulous factory owners and managers made sure that women and children's hours still exceeded those stipulated by the act. It was seen through Parliament by Lord Ashley, later the seventh Earl of Shaftesbury, a Protectionist Tory and a devout Anglican.

There was a scandal in 1846 involving a workhouse in Andover where conditions were found to be appalling. This led to a government review and the abolition of the Poor Law Commission. It was replaced by a Poor Law Board that would be presided over by an MP who would have a position in most governments. Poor law schools were established that were harsh, barracks-like establishments. The Poor Law was also enacted in Ireland, although only in a different form.

A general election was called in 1847 which saw a Conservative victory, but such were the splits in Conservative ranks – between the Protectionists, led by Lord Stanley and the Peelites, led by former Prime Minister, Sir Robert Peel – that they allowed the Whigs, led by Lord John Russell, to continue in office. It was a very confusing election with many factions, even in the same party.

Abroad, it was a dangerous time. Europe was ravaged by a spate of revolutions in 1848. Liberal governments gained temporary office until the old order regained control. In France the Orléans dynasty, with King Louis-Philippe (r. 1830-48) on the throne, was replaced by the Second

Republic. In 1848, Napoleon Bonaparte's nephew, Louis Napoleon, was elected president and, after declaring himself president for life in 1851, was proclaimed as Emperor Napoleon III in 1852. There was political upheaval around the continent, beginning in Sicily in January and spreading from there. There was no coordination but it affected around 50 countries, where people were dissatisfied with the existing political structures and sought more participation in government. Tens of thousands died in the turmoil and many were forced into exile. The revolutions that had an enduring effect occurred in Denmark where absolute monarchy was brought to an end; in Austria, where serfdom was abolished; and in the Netherlands where representative democracy was introduced. In 1848 and 1849, the Habsburg Austrian Empire faced nationalist uprisings as numerous different ethnicities sought independence and autonomy. Meanwhile, in Germany, students and intellectuals demanded national unity, but were eventually defeated.

Britain escaped revolution, although, given the famine in Ireland, the Chartist agitation and the economic depression that occurred in 1847, one might have expected the country to follow suit. There was some agitation – rioting in Glasgow and, in April, a huge Chartist rally at Kennington in London. Feargus O'Connor once again carried a petition to Parliament, this time in a taxi, but the government, mindful of what was occurring abroad, recruited 200,000 special constables, and troops were positioned around London. These actions persuaded radicals that there was little point in trying to create a revolution in Britain.

Britain and the World

Britain continued to enjoy success around the globe, retaining the position of the world's pre-eminent industrial force. In 1830, British exports amounted to £38 million; by 1850, they accounted for £52 million. The main markets for British goods were northern Europe, Canada, the United States, Australia and India but there was growth in places such as Latin America, the Ottoman Empire and the Far East. By the late 1840s, British merchants traded in 1,500 places around the world, more than 60 per cent of them outside Europe.

But people were also leaving Britain to search for a better life elsewhere. Emigration from the UK increased from 700,000 in the 1830s to 1.6 million in the 1840s. Most moved to the United States, but many were beginning to see Canada, Australia and New Zealand as desirable alternatives. Many of the migrants were, of course, Irish, fleeing the horrors of the potato famine but this diaspora helped to establish British influence around the world. So too did the efforts of missionaries who, by the late 1840s, were expanding their global efforts to bring indigenous peoples into the fold. Numerous, mainly London-based missionary societies were sending operatives all over the world, to China, Asia, Africa, India and the Caribbean. This increased pressure on the government to provide support and to claim new territories in which migrants could operate, whether they were traders, missionaries, adventurers or merely seekers of better prospects.

The man responsible for supervision of all of this was Lord Aberdeen (1784-1860) who occupied the role of Foreign Secretary from 1841 to 1846 and would be Prime Minister from 1852 to 1855. He had also been Foreign Secretary in Wellington's government between 1828 and 1830. Occupying the role of Colonial Secretary was Lord Stanley who, like Aberdeen, performed these duties throughout most of Peel's government. Stanley had been Colonial Secretary in Earl Grey's Whig government in 1833 when he had successfully managed the Slavery Abolition Act through Parliament. He had resigned over Ireland in 1834 and resigned from Peel's government over the repeal of the Corn Laws in 1845. These well travelled, well educated, landed peers were also well qualified for their jobs.

The situation they inherited on taking office did not look enticing. The foreign policy of the previous Foreign Secretary, Lord Palmerston, had left Britain in bad odour with both the French and the Americans. Further afield, in China and Afghanistan, things were not a whole lot better.

Palmerston had fallen out with France over the Ottoman Empire, signing the 1840 Convention of London with Austria, Russia and Prussia, without the knowledge of the French. Relations with the United States, meanwhile, were constantly upset by incidents along the Canadian border. In Afghanistan, British forces were under threat from the locals and relations with China over opium had already resulted in armed conflict. As Lord Aberdeen said when he took office:

'In foreign affairs we have enough on our hands; a war with China, a quasi-war in Persia; a state of affairs in the Levant which does not promise a continuance of peace… In addition to all this, our relations with the United States are worse than ever.'

Thus, Aberdeen was faced with a dizzying array of crises around the globe during his time in office. Stanley, meanwhile, made efforts to stabilise British possessions rather than enlarge the empire which would be expensive. He conducted his policy differently to Palmerston, eschewing the gunboat diplomacy that had been employed in China, for instance, and he made strenuous efforts to improve relations with France and the United States. It should be remembered that Britain and the USA had been at war just a few decades earlier and the previous decade had soured the relationship still further when a number of American banking houses collapsed during the economic crisis. The 1833 abolition of slavery in Britain had dismayed the slave-owners of the American South and there was a long-running border dispute between Canada and the United States. Neither did the Royal Navy's policing of the slave trade by patrolling the world's oceans endear Britain to the Americans. This situation, in particular, engendered talk of another war between the two nations. But, Britain's cotton industry was inextricably linked with American production of the crop and war would, therefore, be disastrous. Lord Ashburton (1774-1848) was dispatched to negotiate with the American Secretary of State Daniel Webster (1782-1852) and after lengthy discussion, agreement was reached in autumn 1842.

Dealings with France were smoothed by the good relationship between Aberdeen and French Prime Minister, François Guizot (1787-1874), and were improved still further by a visit to France by Queen Victoria and Prince Albert. King Louis-Philippe and Guizot were pleased to see the *entente cordiale* – the special relationship between France and Great Britain – back on track, French ambitions in various parts of the world notwithstanding. It was necessary in order to forward trade objectives in France, the United States and around the world. War would, of course, have prohibited that.

Afghanistan, India and China

One of Stanley's most pressing tasks when he took office was to deal with a war that had broken out during his predecessor's tenure. British and Indian troops had been under siege in Kabul in Afghanistan for almost two years. They had been sent there by the Governor-General of India, Lord Auckland (1784-1849) in response to growing Russian influence in the region. Their commander, General Elphinstone (1782-1842), was under the misconception that he had safe passage to get his troops out but, in 1842, he and his force of 4,500 were massacred, together with 12,000 civilians, as they beat a retreat from Kabul. Meanwhile, two British political agents in the city – Sir Alexander Burnes (1805-41) and William Macnaghten (1793-1841) – had both been murdered in late 1841 and Emir Shah Shuja (1785-1842) was killed in April 1842. Lord Ellenborough (1790-1871) replaced Auckland as Governor-General and immediately dispatched troops to relieve the beleaguered garrisons at Kandahar and Jalalabad and to bring out the few British troops that remained in Kabul. Once these objectives were achieved, the British forces withdrew, leaving Dost Mohammad (r. 1826-39 and 1845-63) to take the Afghan throne again. Delighted with Ellenborough's decisive action, Stanley resolved to abandon his predecessor's policy of seeking British hegemony in the whole of Asia.

Although Ellenborough was happy not to pursue domination in Afghanistan, this did not mean that he did not have expansionist ambitions elsewhere. Following the withdrawal of British troops from Afghanistan, others began to wonder whether they should continue to support the East India Company and the British. The Emirs of Sind, a province south of Punjab that shared a border with Afghanistan, began to agitate against Britain, leading Ellenborough to send troops under Sir Charles Napier to annex the province. Victorious, Napier famously sent a telegraph to Ellenborough containing one word in Latin – 'Peccavi' which translates as 'I have sinned'. His action alarmed Stanley and the Prime Minister back in London and, when Ellenborough made Gwalior a protected state, they had him withdrawn from his position and replaced by Sir Henry Hardinge (1785-1856). It was too late, however, and the Sikhs of Punjab, dismayed by Britain's recent activity, declared war on the British in December 1845. They were defeated by March 1846, but the treaty that was signed in Lahore served as no more than a brief hiatus before a second conflict broke out.

In the seventeenth and eighteenth centuries, Europeans had an insatiable hunger for Chinese goods such as porcelain, silk and tea. This brought European silver into China, via the southern port of Canton, the only one through which Europeans were allowed to trade. This created a sizeable trade imbalance and, in an effort to counter this, the British East India Company began to auction Indian-grown opium to independent foreign traders in exchange for silver, resulting in massive profits. The effect was to drain Chinese coffers of silver, remove the trade imbalance but also to create an epidemic of opium addiction. In 1839, the Daoguang Emperor (r. 1820-50) banned the trade in opium and closed the port of Canton to foreign merchants. The British government objected to this and a military force was sent to China. In 1840, British troops occupied forts at Cushan and on the Canton River. As Governor-General of India, Ellenborough had influence over what happened in China. When negotiations to bring the war to a conclusion collapsed in January 1841, Stanley was dismayed. The conflict had already cost a great deal, both financially and in terms of lives lost. He wanted it to end, but Ellenborough instead encouraged General Sir Hugh Gough (1779-1869) to continue prosecuting the conflict. British troops captured Shanghai and advanced along the Yangtze River, at great cost in terms of the lives of Chinese civilians and soldiers. Angered at Ellenborough's expensive imperialist ambitions, Stanley wrote to him: 'There is little advantage and no glory in such affairs as the wholesale slaughter, without loss on our part, of Chinese...' He urged Ellenborough 'to close, whether by treaty or by retaining possession of such parts as we have got and choose to keep, this unfortunate war'.

As we have already noted, Stanley preferred to maintain

relations with the Chinese Emperor and to create favourable trading conditions rather than expand British territory in China. It would cost too much to maintain, anyway. He would happily have given up British possession of Hong Kong for these reasons, but military, mercantile and political opinion was that the island should be annexed. In August 1842, with British troops at the gates of Nanking, the emperor decided to end the war and the Treaty of Nanking was signed. Stanley was unhappy when he saw the terms of the treaty, however. Ellenborough and Gough had secured Hong Kong for Britain. But the treaty also opened three Chinese ports to trade as well as Canton and Shanghai. British goods would now enjoy a 5 per cent tariff and China agreed to pay Britain the sum of £21 million. Following the war, China slid into a period of turmoil and bloodshed that was only brought to an end, a century later, by the 1949 Communist victory. A Second Opium War, won by Britain and France, followed between 1856 and 1860 and China would for a long time be weakened and exploited by Europeans and the Japanese, a period that became known as the 'hundred years of humiliation'.

As Colonial Secretary, Stanley did his best to rein in the imperialist, expansionist forces. By 1848, however, several years after he departed this role, his worst fears were being realised. The British Empire was struggling, relying far too much on multi-ethnic peasant armies that were funded by unpopular local taxes. This was especially the case in the

Indian subcontinent and in Southern Africa. Unprecedented amounts of money were also being spent on maintaining garrisons and on the administration of the colonies, and British rule was guaranteed by force in almost the entire empire. It was unsustainable.

A New Government

It had been Peel's ambition that the repeal of the Corn Laws would reduce the antipathy to aristocratic government. It had one unintended result, however – a split in the Conservative Party that would last for a generation. Staunch protectionists, such as Lord Stanley and Disraeli, were horrified by the repeal of the Corn Laws and Peel's 1829 position on Catholic emancipation. He did have his followers, however, men such as Lord Aberdeen and Gladstone, for whom the Tory Party no longer provided a home but who could never become Whigs. Westminster's old two-party politics no longer applied, leaving the Tories able only to form minority governments. Meanwhile, coalitions between radicals, Whigs, those who called themselves Liberals and the followers of Peel were inherently precarious. Peel never again held public office but for the few years he had left, he was worshipped by the middle and working classes for improving their lot and introducing difficult reforms. When he died, aged just 62, after being thrown from his horse in July 1850, there was an outpouring of national grief.

Peel was followed as Prime Minister by the Whig Lord John Russell, his party coming to power principally because of the split on the other side of the House. The son of a Duke himself, Russell filled his cabinet with aristocrats but it proved to be a difficult task to manage such a collection of grandees. In the general election of 1847, the Whigs and Liberals won a small majority and Russell would hang on to power until 1852, mainly due to the disarray in the Conservative Party. In 1847, as we have seen, his government passed a new Factory Act that limited to ten the hours that women and children could work. To get the act through the House, the Whigs allied themselves with the Tory Protectionists while Peelites and the Liberals – factory owners and manufacturers – inveighed against it, fearing falling production figures and a consequent reduction in profits. The following year brought a Public Health Act that had been championed by Sir Edwin Chadwick. The government was forced to enact compromises before it was passed but it was a significant piece of legislation, the first to concern itself with the health and welfare of the entire nation. It established a General Board of Health which had an inspectorate to ensure that sanitary policy was applied by town councils and locally established boards of health. In 1849, the mid-seventeenth-century Navigation Acts were rescinded. These stipulated that all goods imported into

Britain should be carried by British vessels and represented one of the last barriers – along with the repeal of the Corn Laws – to the establishment of free trade. Such legislative moves, ardently opposed by Protectionists, entailed a high degree of wheeling and dealing.

These were once again difficult times. The British economy took a downward turn as 'railway mania' faded and shares in railways collapsed late in 1845. A severe financial crisis in 1847 closed many factories and mills, and unemployment was severe in the north and the Midlands. Another run of poor harvests took the price of corn to 100 shillings a quarter and huge quantities of grain had to be imported, depleting the country's precious reserves of gold. Government revenue fell dramatically.

Although Britain managed to escape the revolutionary activity sweeping Europe, there were crises in the wider British Empire. Rioting and rebellion broke out in Malta, Ceylon (modern-day Sri Lanka) and the Ionian Islands; there was trouble in Montreal in Canada where the Parliament building was set on fire, and in the Cape in Southern Africa; and in New South Wales and Van Diemen's Land in Australia, settlers protested against the increased numbers of convicts who were being transported to their territories. Financial crises, too, crippled a number of colonies such as British Guiana and Jamaica, where the authorities were forced to suspend all public spending.

The news of revolution abroad yet again revived the Chartists. In spring 1848, a new petition was begun. A demonstration was organised on Kennington Common and 10 April was named as the day for the presentation of a third petition but it was all to no avail. Parliament once again rejected the points in the petition, bringing the Chartist movement to an end once and for all.

Good Riddance to the 'Hungry Forties'?

The decade had ended as harshly as it had begun, despite Peel's best efforts to improve things. Writers and intellectuals did not hesitate to criticise the state of contemporary British society. Whether in Emily Bronte's (1818-48) *Wuthering Heights* (1847) or her sister Charlotte's (1816-55) *Jane Eyre* (1847), the divided nation and its patriarchal society were laid bare. Charles Dickens published *Dombey and Son* in 1848, taking aim at cruelty towards children and the blight of the arranged marriage for financial gain. The agricultural system that ensured so many farm workers withered in desperate poverty was condemned by Charles Kingsley (1819-75) in *Yeast* (1848). The plight of workers in Manchester was highlighted by Elizabeth Gaskell's (1810-65) *Mary Barton* (1848) and William Makepeace Thackeray's (1811-63) books, *Vanity Fair* and *Pendennis* criticised the upper classes for their sloth and hypocrisy.

There were some good things, too, of course. Teacher, inventor and social reformer, Sir Rowland Hill (1795-1879) had campaigned for the reform of the postal system, championing the idea of the Uniform Penny Post. Prepayment, he reasoned, would create an efficient and safe way for letters to be moved around the country. The early years of the decade, therefore, saw the introduction of the postage stamp. The commercial Christmas card first appeared in 1843, commissioned by the British civil servant and inventor, Sir Henry Cole (1808-82), and illustrated by John Callcott Horsley (1817-1903). William Henry Fox Talbot (1800-77) in the 1840s did pioneering work in the new field of photography.

In the world of art, the influential Pre-Raphaelite Brotherhood was founded by William Holman Hunt (1827-1910), Dante Gabriel Rossetti (1828-82) and John Everett Millais (1829-96) in 1848. The group aimed to reform art by returning to the artistic principles that existed before the Italian Renaissance painter, Raphael. The group objected in particular to the work of Sir Joshua Reynolds which they believed was the antithesis of everything art should stand for.

One particularly significant figure in the 1840s was the MP and essayist, Thomas Babington Macaulay (1800-59) whose reputation had been gained from his wonderful writing for the periodical, the *Edinburgh Review*. As a member of the Supreme Council of India from 1834 to 1838, Macaulay had been influential in Indian affairs. In that role, he had come to support the reforms proposed by William Bentinck and, in his *Minute on Indian Education*, he supported the notion of providing a western-style education for South Asians. This, he promised, would produce an entirely new class of Indian – one 'English in tastes, in opinions, in morals and in intellect' who would still be Indian in 'blood and colour'. These people, he argued, would be perfectly suited to mediating between the British Raj and the wider Indian population. Returning from India, Macaulay became a full-time writer, compiling the *Lays of Ancient Rome* in 1842, a sequence of narrative poems that retold the heroic stories of Rome. Espousing the values of patriotism, courage and self-sacrifice, these would colour the lives of English public schoolboys for generations to come. He briefly became an MP, but lost his seat in the election of 1847. In 1848, his *History of England*, a work infused with optimism about Britain, was a bestseller. Life for him, at least, at the end of the 1840s, was not too bad.

3

The 1850s:
The 'Age of Equipoise'

'The Strong Arm of England'

Since Napoleon's defeat at the Battle of Waterloo in 1815, Britain had experienced a sequence of debilitating downturns, but the crash of the late 1840s would prove to be the last for some time. In fact, it would be the turning-point for the Victorians, as Chartist agitation died away and the restlessness of the working class dissipated. Stability became the new norm, the agreements with the French and the Americans were firmly in place and there was calm in Europe after the traumas of 1848. Britain felt that she had dodged a bullet, as it were, and was in a good position to deal with the second half of the nineteenth century.

Lord Palmerston was in the Foreign Office again at this point, and reaping the benefits of the drastic change of mood not only at home, but around the world. He was the most experienced of Russell's cabinet, a somewhat difficult man who had held public office since the early 1800s and who had already been Foreign Secretary, as we have seen, during the 1830s. His task, as he saw it, was to repair what had been wrought by his predecessor, Lord Aberdeen, who he thought had done little but appease and accommodate. Instead, Palmerston returned to the type of gunboat diplomacy that had served him well in the past.

In what became known as the 'Don Pacifico Affair', he sent British vessels to Greece after a British subject had been victim of an anti-Semitic attack. His actions were debated and criticised in Parliament for five days but he delivered a bravura speech that destroyed any disapproval of him. It dealt with the type of country Britain was and why it had survived during the European turbulence of the late 1840s:

'We have shown the example of a nation in which every class of society accepts with cheerfulness the lot which Providence has assigned to it; while at the same time each individual of each class is constantly trying to raise himself in the social scale – not by injustice and wrong, not by violence and illegality, but by persevering good conduct, and by the steady and energetic exertion of the moral and intellectual faculties with which his creator has endowed him.'

When it came time to vote, he won easily, by 310 to 264. But his speech, boasting of 'the strong arm of England', was idealistic and arrogant, one that bespoke the ruling elite and came nowhere near to describing the reality of British society at the time. Of course, 'the lot that Providence had generally assigned' most British people was far from acceptable to them. Many remained in poverty and unemployment, maimed by war or exploited by technology. In Palmerston's narrative, Britain was stable and contented at home and unassailable overseas, but, of course, this was arrant nonsense, as would be proved in the decade that followed.

In another incident, Palmerston earned the outrage of Queen Victoria when, in September 1850, during a visit to Britain, the detested Austrian General Julius Jacob von Haynau (1786-1853) was set upon by a group of brewery workers and chased down Borough High Street in London. They were disgusted by his brutality during the 1848 revolution which had earned him the sobriquet the 'Hangman of Arad'. The Queen demanded that the government should apologise to Austria and Palmerston was directed to write an official apology. It was obvious, however, from what he said that he had more sympathy with the workers than with the general. Queen Victoria already disliked Palmerston and, angered by his speech, she unsuccessfully sought his resignation.

He was finally pressured into resigning by Russell in December 1851 after he announced the government's approval of Louis Napoleon Bonaparte's abolition of the French Republic. His announcement had neither the approval of the Cabinet nor Russell.

The State of the Nation

The census of 1841 provided more information about the population of Britain than any in previous years. The first had been staged in 1801, but the one in 1841 was the first that was truly national, supervised for the whole country by a central body. It delved into details of people's lives beyond just names and numbers, asking for birth, age, marital status and what a person's relation was to the head of the household. An unprecedented religious census was also carried out in England and Wales but with less enthusiasm in Scotland and not at all in Ireland. No similar exercise has been carried out since. A third census investigated educational provision in the middle of the nineteenth century. It attempted to find out how many children were attending school and the nature of the schools they were attending.

Britain's education, behaviour and sociology were changing. The population of the entire country – Great Britain and Ireland – was 27 million, a population that would have seemed unsustainable a few decades earlier. The population of England and Wales had almost doubled since 1801 and the same was true of Scotland which had three million inhabitants. In Ireland, following the famine, the number of inhabitants declined from more than eight million in the 1841 census to six and a half million just ten years later. In contrast to the remainder of Britain and the rest of Europe, the population of Ireland would continue to decline for the rest of the nineteenth century. For the first time, the majority of the English population was shown to live in towns and cities, although, in the other countries of the Union, people remained largely rural dwellers. In Scotland, just one third of the population lived in an urban setting, mostly in Edinburgh, Glasgow and in the area between the two cities. The largest city in Wales turned out to be Merthyr Tydfil but its inhabitants numbered only 50,000. Today's large cities of Cardiff and Swansea came nowhere close.

Therefore, despite the radical changes in the British economy since the census was first introduced, the 'workshop of the world' was not that industrialised. More people – around two million, and mostly men – worked in agriculture than in factories. Domestic service accounted for around a million, and there were just over half a million cotton textile workers evenly split between the sexes. In numerical order after these came builders, labourers, milliners, dressmakers, and seamstresses of whom there were about a third of a million. Woollen workers numbered 300,000 – both male and female –

while there were just over 200,000 coalminers. Things had not radically changed. More people worked with horses on the roads than worked with steam engines; there were more blacksmiths than those employed in ironworks; and the number employed in the textile industry was less than those employed in agriculture.

It was certainly true that the lot of the average British person had seen little improvement as a result of the first stages of the Industrial Revolution. Ireland, of course, had been disadvantaged by not having undergone any type of industrialisation and famine and the subsequent decimation of the population by starvation and emigration was the inevitable result. Generally, in Britain, the individual lived what the economist John Stuart Mill (1806-73) described as 'the same life of drudgery and imprisonment' while his or her employer made a fortune.

Religion remained a significant feature in British life in the mid-nineteenth century as the religious census hoped to prove. It sought to find out how many people in England, Wales and Scotland attended church services on a given day, 30 March. There was no attempt to find out the religious affiliation of the entire population of these three parts of Britain but it was shown that of the people who could have attended church on that particular Sunday, only half did. Fifty per cent of those attended Church of England services and the others attended dissenting places of worship or were Catholics. It was evident that many of the lower classes had no religious inclinations, and it must have disappointed Anglicans to learn that the same number attended dissenting chapels as did their churches. Only a quarter of the population adhered to the faith of the established Church of the country. On the plus side, the Anglican Church remained the largest denomination and 80 per cent of all marriages in the country were conducted by Anglican vicars. In Scotland, church attendance was higher on a percentage basis than in England and Wales, and the established Presbyterian Church was the largest denomination. As with England and Wales, Catholics represented only a small minority.

The population census demonstrated that, although Britain was the most technologically advanced nation on the face of the earth, industry still fell behind agriculture in terms of the numbers it employed; the religious census that despite our claims to be a Christian nation, most people did not worship in the established church or did not worship at all; and the education census informed us that we were also under-educated, as a nation. The latter, however, was not an exact science, as many schools refused to supply the information required. The official who was responsible for the censuses, Horace Mann, estimated that the average British child spent almost five years at school, implying that the children of upper- and middle-class parents spent perhaps six years being educated while working-class children were in school for little more than four years. In his report he cheerfully concluded that 'very few children are *completely* uninstructed'. He suggested that around 80 per cent of children attended school, but evidence would suggest that this figure was closer to 50 per cent.

Britain had welcomed many refugees from the turmoil of Europe in 1848 but their lives were hard. Amongst the notable revolutionaries and agitators who had made London their home were Louis Blanc (1811-82), a French champion of cooperatives that would guarantee that the poor had employment; the German Karl Marx who had been ordered out of Prussia in 1843 and six years later fled Paris where he was seen as a political threat; Giuseppe Mazzini (1805-72), a fervent activist for the unification of Italy; Lajos Kossuth (1802-94), a Hungarian nobleman who had briefly been Regent-President of Hungary following the 1848 revolution; and the Sicilian independence fighters, the Scalia brothers, Luigi and Alfonso. There were also numerous exiles from Czarist Russia and Poland. From the other side of the revolutionary fence, London was also home to men such as King Louis-Philippe of France and Prince Metternich (1773-1859) who had been Chancellor of Austria. There were those who were very proud of Britain's policy of welcoming exiles from the Continent, but there were, of course, also those who bristled at the thought of agitators and revolutionaries walking the streets of the capital.

Victorian Morality

The term 'Victorian morality' has come to denote a set of values that advocates sexual restraint, low tolerance of crime and a rigid social code of conduct. These were the values that the British believed they had a moral obligation to take to the countries that had been brought into the British Empire. One outward indicator of the morality the Victorians espoused was the abolition of slavery throughout the British Empire, an act passed just four years before Queen Victoria ascended the throne. The Royal Navy patrolled the high seas, stopping ships suspected of carrying slaves and freeing them. Freed slaves were transported to Sierra Leone, a Crown Colony in West Africa established for just this purpose.

When we speak of Victorian morality, however, it is usually the Victorian attitude to sex to which we are referring. Religion undoubtedly played a large part in this, the evangelicals in the Nonconformist movement as well as in the Church of England insisting on 'proper' behaviour and establishing organisations to monitor that and lobby government for action to promote it.

Victorian times saw a definite decline in many insalubrious practices such as gambling, horse racing and obscene theatres. Patronage of brothels fell and the debauched behaviour of English aristocrats that had been commonplace in the eighteenth century was consigned to history. It is especially true that the middle class – a class that grew in numbers as well as power towards the end of the Victorian era – espoused high moral standards. This was thought to be less true of the working class, living in overcrowded slums, living out of wedlock and giving birth to illegitimate children. Recent research, however, has suggested that this was less common than originally thought.

Prostitution had, of course, been widespread in cities throughout history but campaigners began to agitate seriously on this issue in the 1840s. Known as 'The Great Social Evil', it was subject to campaigns by the press, clergymen, and single women. It is estimated that there were 8,600 prostitutes working in London alone in 1857. Institutions were opened to try to save what were known as 'fallen women'. The 'fallen woman' became a staple of mid-Victorian literature, a person who had been corrupted or soiled and who needed cleansing. She was seen as a destroyer of the myth of the woman as a home-maker, creating a space for her husband and family that was free of the noise, filth and corruption of the city outside. At the same time, men who visited prostitutes were not considered to be part of the problem, perpetuating what had long been a double standard in sexual morality. This double standard, as has been noted, was also prevalent in divorce law where a man could divorce his wife for one act of adultery, but a woman could divorce for adultery only if it was combined with another offence such as incest, cruelty, bigamy, desertion and so on.

Moral reform organisations and movements worked to close down brothels which, it has been argued, served to drive women onto the streets to ply their trade. The Jack the Ripper murders in London in the 1880s brought the extent of the problem to global prominence when five prostitutes were brutally slain in London's East End.

Homosexual acts were made illegal in the Labouchère Amendment to the Criminal Law Amendment Act of 1885. This punished convicted males with two years' imprisonment, whether their acts were in public or in private. Female same-sex acts were not subject to similar treatment, since lesbianism was thought at the time to be virtually non-existent. Of course, the most famous victim of the Labouchère Amendment was the playwright, Oscar Wilde, imprisoned in 1895 for sodomy and gross indecency.

Protestants and Catholics

In 1850, Pope Pius IX (in office 1846-78) decided to make changes to the Catholic hierarchy in England and reinstate dioceses. Since the Reformation, bishops had been replaced by vicars apostolic. There was outrage across the country at what was viewed as papal interference in British matters and the subservience of the Catholic

Church in England to Rome. The change was, in reality, the idea of Nicholas Wiseman (1802-65), head of the Catholic Church in England who was made a cardinal in the new hierarchy. At the time, Catholicism was on the rise. Numbers were growing in cities such as Glasgow and Liverpool which had taken in a great many Irish Catholics during and after the famine. The flames of anger had been fanned by the conversion to Catholicism of High Church Anglicans and members of the High Church Oxford Movement such as the theologian and poet John Henry Newman (1801-90) who converted in 1845. With other prominent Anglicans doing likewise, it was feared that the Church of England was being undermined by a resurgent Catholic Church. Thus, the Pope's decision to restructure the English Catholic Church, with the first bishops being appointed in 1850, caused a great deal of alarm. At the top of the hierarchy was the newly created position of Archbishop of Westminster and bishoprics did not follow the geographic designations used by the Anglican Church. In this way, the Pope hoped that he would not be treading on Anglican toes. It made no difference, however, and the situation was made worse by the news that Lord John Russell, the Prime Minister, who had earlier been supportive, had now switched allegiance and was throwing in his lot with the protesters. In 1851, he passed the anti-Catholic Ecclesiastical Titles Act that, somewhat ridiculously, prevented the Roman Catholic

Church from using the same names for its bishoprics as the Anglican Church. As the Pope had very deliberately avoided doing this, the bill was pointless and was repealed in 1871.

The High Tide of the Victorian Age

The end of Russell's government in 1852 came about on a confidence vote, driven, ironically, by Palmerston. An amendment he proposed on a militia bill won a majority in the Commons, bringing down the government and providing the former Foreign Secretary the revenge he desired for his loss of office just a few months previously. It was a significant moment because it could be argued that the last few years of the Russell government represented a high point in Victorian Britain. Indeed, commentators have often noted how much of a contrast there was between the tumultuous first half of the nineteenth century, culminating, as it did, in the 'hungry forties' and the second half of the century, a period of relative calm and stability. In the second half of the century, there were few civil disturbances and none of the political agitation stirred up by reform and Chartism. Neither was there industrial unrest nor protests such as those staged by the Luddites and the general strike of 1842, nor rural disturbances such as the Swing Riots. It has been described by some commentators as the 'age of equipoise'.

That change was in the air at this mid-point of the century, however, was perhaps signalled by the passing in 1852 of the Duke of Wellington who was laid to rest in a magnificent state funeral. Alfred Tennyson (1809-92) who had taken the role of Poet Laureate on the recent death of the previous incumbent, William Wordsworth (1770-1850), and would remain in the position until his own death in 1892, wrote in his 'Ode on the Death of the Duke of Wellington':

> Lead out the pageant: sad and slow,
> As fits an universal woe,
> Let the long long procession go,
> And let the sorrowing crowd about it grow,
> And let the mournful martial music blow;
> The last great Englishman is low.

Of course, there was a certain irony in his being called 'the last great Englishman' because his ancestry was Anglo-Irish but he was undoubtedly a great hero as evidenced by the grandeur of his funeral, directed by Prince Albert and watched by one and a half million people lining the streets of London. For many, a great age had passed that had been peopled with giants, great men who strode the world stage like kings and those who took their place were no match for them. The irony was that this feeling of decline coincided with a period in which many had never had it so good.

In 1851, Prince Albert, Henry Cole and others organised what was effectively the first world's fair at Hyde Park in London. Dubbed the Great Exhibition, it was staged in a unique building, largely made of glass and known as the Crystal Palace, which would later be dismantled and rebuilt in south London. It brought exhibits and displays from around the world, showcased industry, innovation and invention and also brought visitors from many parts of the globe – about six million of them between May and October 1851. Amongst the British visitors were many poor people who had previously never left their home town, let alone come to London. The exhibition's aim was to emphasise Britain's position as industrial leader.

When it had first been proposed a Royal Commission had been formed to investigate its viability and, indeed, many Conservatives had been against the idea. They had feared that it would be a source of unrest amongst the people of Britain. In fact, one famously reactionary and much lampooned Tory MP, Colonel Charles de Laet Waldo Sibthorp (1783-1855), had railed against the 'foreign assassins and venereal disease' that he feared the exhibition would bring to London.

But, after its opening by Queen Victoria, the exhibition was a huge success. The *Times* described the opening as 'the first morning since the creation of the world that all peoples have assembled from all parts of the world and done a common act'. More than 100,000 exhibits from around the globe were on display, provided by 14,000 individual and corporate lenders. They were divided into four distinct categories – raw materials; machinery; manufactured goods; and the fine arts. It is estimated that by its final day, it had been seen by around 20 per cent of the population of Britain, especially after it was announced that on certain days entry would cost only a shilling, making it affordable for more than the elite. Special trains were also laid on, bringing visitors from around the country.

There was one particular legacy of the Great Exhibition that is worthy of note. The surplus cash that it generated was invested in the acquisition of land in South Kensington. On that site were built the Victoria and Albert Museum, the Natural History Museum and the Science Museum. The Imperial College of Science and Technology and the Royal Albert Hall were also constructed. This all represented the singular contribution of Prince Albert to the land that he had adopted, a contribution probably unmatched by any member of the British royal family since.

It seemed that Britain was in a sustained period of progress and prosperity. Internationally, competitors had been left far behind. Ten times more coal was consumed in Britain than in France and six times more than in the regions that would eventually become Germany. Britain turned out and consumed iron in quantities three or four times greater than elsewhere and many more steam engines were in use than anywhere else. Despite the size of Germany and France, Britain had constructed more railway lines than in those two countries combined. Britain produced half the world's pig-iron, half the world's coal and in its mills and factories almost 50 per cent of the world's production of raw cotton was consumed. In 1851, British gross domestic product per capita was 65 per cent higher than that of Germany and 30 per cent more than that of the Netherlands or the United States.

Interestingly, however, in the middle of the nineteenth century, despite its unrivalled position as the world's industrial superpower, Britain's military might was inadequate. The funds were simply not there for Peel, Russell or even later, Gladstone, as a result of debt accumulated in the Revolutionary and Napoleonic Wars. Thus, public expenditure was constantly under pressure in the decades that followed, no more than 2 or 3 per cent of gross national product being diverted to the army and the navy. Much more was spent in the previous century and in the one following. The 65,000 troops of the British army simply could not compete with the other European powers. Prussia had 127,000; Russia 900,000; France 324,000; and the Habsburg Empire boasted 400,000. In terms of military technology and innovation, Britain had also fallen far behind its European rivals. Taking part in any conflict in Europe, therefore, was out of the question even though British strategic interests were constantly under threat in the Iberian Peninsula, the Dardanelles and Belgium, for instance. In the empire, however, there were British soldiers. There was also the Indian army to support them, 300,000 strong and costing the British taxpayer nothing. The Indian army was used in East Africa, the Middle East and China, but the number of troops was regarded by British officials overseas and military heads as inadequate, given the vast areas in which they operated.

The Royal Navy was in a much better position, being larger than any other navy. It kept fleets in the North Sea and in the Mediterranean and still acted as a policeman on the oceans of the world, ensuring that trade routes were secure by fighting piracy and stopping vessels engaged in the slave trade. Even so, the navy still had to endure a reduction in size and it was run on a shoestring. It was just as well that tensions had decreased since 1815 and the end of the Napoleonic Wars. There was no longer the global scramble for empire, and France and Spain had withdrawn from overseas expansion. Russia's efforts to gain ground in Asia did not often trouble Britain and it would be several decades before Germany would come to the fore as a global power.

A New Type of Politics

With the demise of Lord John Russell's government in 1852, a new style of politics was born. Throughout the

1830s and the 1840s, party divisions between Whig-Liberals and Tory-Conservatives were very clear. Now, those certainties were thrown in the air. There was also concern about the country's place in the world and whether it could hang on to its empire much longer. There were new rivals on the scene, such as the United States, placing British overseas possessions under threat – especially, of course, Canada. Britain resolved to defend its North American territory as well as the Antipodes and South Africa. Some even suggested that the way to hold it all together would be in some form of imperial federation. For those who felt it was the God-given right of the British to rule the world and to take its religion to its peoples, there was the dismay of realising that the empire consisted of many different religious denominations – Catholics in Ireland and Canada, adherents of the Dutch Reformed Church in South Africa and, of course, Muslims and Hindus in British India. The subcontinent provided by far the largest community in the empire and missionary efforts there were doomed to failure. The British Empire was no longer mostly Protestant. The belief that it was preordained that the British would reign supreme around the world and that the peoples of subjugated nations would have no hesitation in converting to Christianity was not tenable.

Following the long death of Russell's government, the Earl of Derby (the former Lord Stanley) formed the first of three Conservative governments over which he presided.

Derby would be leader of the Conservative Party for an astounding 22 years, the longest-serving leader to date. He came from a wealthy family, was a respected classical scholar and a brilliant debater. Entering Parliament in 1820 as a Whig, and serving in a junior capacity under Earl Grey when the Reform Bill was passed, he fell out with the government over its reforms in the Church of Ireland in 1834 and resigned. Embracing the Reformist cause, he joined the Conservatives and was appointed Colonial Secretary under Peel in 1841. The repeal of the Corn Laws was a step too far for him, however, and he resigned once more. He became the leader of the Tory Protectionist faction in 1846.

When he tried to form a cabinet, he discovered that he did not have much with which to work, because the real talent in the party maintained loyalty to Peel. Thus, his government earned the sobriquet of the 'Who? Who? Ministry' because no one knew who these new ministers were. The name came from the Duke of Wellington who, very deaf by this time, was said to have responded 'Who?' to every name that he was given of new cabinet members. Spencer Walpole (1806-98) who was appointed Home Secretary and would occupy that position three times under the Earl of Derby, had only entered Parliament in 1847. The Foreign Secretary, Lord Malmesbury (1807-89), admitted he had little experience for the job but his friendship with Louis Napoleon Bonaparte, who had been in exile in London from 1836 to 1840, would prove relatively useful. Secretary of State for War and the Colonies was the relatively unknown Sir John Pakington (1799-1880). The most surprising appointment was that of Benjamin Disraeli as Chancellor of the Exchequer, a position for which, it was felt, he was completely unsuited, given that he knew nothing of finance and his own finances were often a mess. A writer of somewhat derivative novels, Disraeli was regarded as a bit of an adventurer. Born a Jew but a convert to Anglicanism, he broke with the Conservative tradition by attending neither public school nor university. He was disliked intensely by Peelites due to his scathing attacks in Parliament on Robert Peel in the late 1840s. These were made on behalf of the Tory landowners and adherents to High Anglicanism, but they did not much like him either because he was a maverick who did not fall into their image of what a politician should be. He had no aristocratic family associations and owned no land until later in life. They had preferred George Bentinck as their leader in the House. After Bentinck's death in 1848, Lord Granby (1815-88), later Duke of Rutland, took on the role. At the time, Disraeli was unacceptable to the Earl of Derby, leader of the party. Eventually, Disraeli took over leadership of the Conservative Party in the Commons in 1852 and he would occupy that role unopposed until 1876.

The election that brought Derby to power took place in July 1852 and came to represent something of a watershed in British politics. It was evident that the Tory-Conservative Party was now becoming the party of the rural aristocracy while the Whig-Liberal party was supported by the rising urban bourgeoisie. The election was extremely close, both in terms of the numbers of seats each party won and the share of the popular vote. The Conservatives won 330 seats to the Whigs' 324; the former received 430,882 votes, the latter 311,481. The split between the Peelites and the Protectionist Tories, however, had made the formation of a majority government very difficult.

Disraeli's first budget tried to be conciliatory towards everyone. For the landowners and the agricultural faction, he reduced the tax on malt; for the radicals, he introduced different levels of tax for earned and unearned income. The budget was full of trickery in the way he presented the figures and Gladstone made short work of it in the speech he delivered in response. It was rejected by 305 votes to 285 and, after less than a year in office, the Earl of Derby's first government was forced to resign.

Thus did one of the great political rivalries in British Parliamentary history begin and it would continue until 1881, ended only by Disraeli's death. Both men were originally Conservatives. Disraeli would remain a Tory, despite his rupture with Peel and his policies; Gladstone, on the other hand, was unstintingly loyal to Peel and his trajectory would have an entirely different destination. He would eventually become the leader of the party that emerged from the Whigs, radicals and Peelites – the Liberal Party. Queen Victoria would later say of him that she would:

> 'sooner abdicate than send for or have any *communication* with that half-mad fire-brand who would soon ruin everything and be a *Dictator*.'

All of the recent Prime Ministers – Aberdeen, Russell, Derby and Palmerston – had been born in the late eighteenth century. Disraeli was born at the start of the nineteenth, as were Gladstone, Prince Albert and Queen Victoria. It was the changing of the guard.

Aberdeen's Coalition

After 1846, everything had changed. Neither of the two main parties was able to command the majority in Parliament that was needed to govern without the help of another party. This, of course, led to compromise and the watering-down of policies. The radicals, the Peelites and the Irish assumed a great deal of influence in this situation. They shared a deep antipathy to both the Whigs who were against any further reform and the Conservatives who continued to champion the Church of England. Governments rose and fell, therefore, not on the votes of the electorate but on the whim of MPs. This constant changing of the government left space for Albert and Victoria to dip in and out of politics as and when they wanted. Thus, when Derby's government fell in December 1852, they asked Lord Aberdeen to form a coalition of Peelites – the grouping he had led since 1846 – as well as Whigs, Liberals and radicals. Aberdeen had already come to an agreement with Lord John Russell earlier in the year and a cabinet was created that consisted of 6 Peelites, 6 Whigs and 1 radical. It was a good deal for the Peelites as the Whigs had more MPs than them. Russell was Foreign Secretary and Palmerston was given the Home Office. The Peelite Gladstone accepted the job of Chancellor.

All did not go well from the very beginning, however. Inevitably, the Whigs were disgruntled at the Peelite presence in the cabinet, given that the Whigs were numerically stronger in the Commons. There were also personal conflicts, however. Russell and Palmerston did not get on and Aberdeen also had problems with Palmerston. Russell felt short-changed by his negotiations with Aberdeen and also believed that he was the equal of the Prime Minister, a view that Aberdeen certainly did not share. He also thought Aberdeen had promised to make way for him sometime in the future, but Aberdeen remained vague about this. In February 1853, therefore, Russell resigned from the Foreign Office, being replaced by Lord Clarendon (1800-70). Russell had more minor government jobs from that point on and Aberdeen continued to hold onto the premiership.

Despite the unsettled nature of the coalition and especially the conflict between its three main players, there were some achievements. The first of these was Gladstone's first budget. Recent budgets had been derided by the Peelites. Russell had spent the surplus the government had on relief following the Irish Potato Famine, expenditure that they felt was wasted. And Disraeli's budget was obviously anathema to them. Gladstone resolved that his budget, delivered in 1853, would show sound fiscal sense and display prudent management of public funds. He departed from convention by announcing plans for the next seven years. Peel had re-introduced income tax as what he claimed was a temporary measure in 1842, and Gladstone stuck to this claim, committing to reductions until it would be abolished completely by 1860. The economy at the time was such that this could be achieved. It was further enabled by healthy government revenues in the early years of the decade. It was a stroke of genius and put Gladstone's name firmly on the map as the brightest star amongst the younger generation of politicians. His five-hour speech demonstrated his responsible financial management but also his complete mastery of the Commons.

Palmerston also performed well in his new role, passing a new Factory Act in 1853 that rendered it illegal for young people to work between the hours of 6 pm and 6 am. His

Truck Act prevented the practice of employers paying their workers in goods instead of money or compelling them to use shops owned by employers. His 1853 Smoke Abatement Act tried to reduce the amount of smoke from coal fires that was polluting the atmosphere and he persuaded the government to put its weight behind the 1853 Vaccination Act that, for the first time, made vaccination of children compulsory. He reduced the time a prisoner could be held in solitary confinement from eighteen months to nine months and in the Penal Servitude Act of 1853, brought an end to the transportation of convicts to Van Diemen's Land (modern-day Tasmania). That act also reduced the maximum sentences for almost every offence. His Reformatory School Act of 1854 allowed the Home Secretary the power to send juvenile prisoners to a reformatory school instead of prison. Palmerston was also responsible for the Northcote-Trevelyan Report. This led ultimately to the creation of a professional, incorruptible and impartial civil service in Britain that took people on and promoted them on merit rather than on who they were or what family they belonged to. A competitive examination was recommended but it would not be until 1870 that these ideas came to fruition. Palmerston opposed further reform of the electoral system and, when the cabinet decided in December 1853 to introduce a bill in the next session, extending the franchise to the urban working class, he resigned. Aberdeen persuaded him to stay in his role by convincing him that no definite decision about reform had yet been taken.

These were not the great causes that had inflamed passions in the 1830s and 1840s and Lord John Russell soon became frustrated, to the extent that he once again took up the cudgel of reform, proposing a further expansion of the franchise. He put forward a bill in 1852 and another in 1854, but there was little enthusiasm, either in Parliament or amongst the general public. Neither was successful.

The Crimean War

The most important event during the Aberdeen government of the early 1850s was the Crimean War, the only really significant war in which Britain participated between the Battle of Waterloo in 1815 and the conflict with the Boers in South Africa in 1899. Its origins lay in an unlikely issue – the rights of Christian minorities in the Holy Land which at the time was part of the Ottoman Empire. Custody of the holy places in Bethlehem and Jerusalem had long been shared by monks of the Greek Orthodox Church and Roman Catholic priests but had in recent times been exercised only by the Greek Orthodox representatives. This greatly displeased Napoleon III of France. But, of course, the dispute was about a lot more than this immediate issue. It was also about the Ottoman Empire and its vast territories, control of the eastern Mediterranean, and Russia's expansionist aspirations in the Near East and possibly India as well. Russia was deeply unpopular at the time in Britain because of its ruler, Czar Nicholas I (r. 1825-55), and his autocratic style of government. His harsh treatment of Russian reformers outraged British liberals while those of a more conservative bent were suspicious of the Czar's territorial ambitions. His country was already being described as 'a prison house of nations', a reference to the conquered nations that were being forced to be part of the Russian Empire.

In 1853, Russia invaded Romania, at the time a province of Turkey, ostensibly to protect the rights of Orthodox Christians in the region. Turkey responded by declaring war on Russia in October of that year. In the first real action a month later, a squadron of Turkish vessels was defeated by ships of the Imperial Russian fleet in the Battle of Sinop in the Black Sea. In the British press this incident was presented as a massacre. A month later, in December 1853, Britain and France agreed to join together to fight Russian expansion in Turkey. The immediate aim was to prevent the Russian navy from leaving harbour at Sebastopol on the Black Sea in order to seize the Turkish capital, Constantinople (modern-day Istanbul). Ultimatums and diplomatic withdrawals ensued and war was declared by the two European powers on 28 March 1854. It would be recognised as one of the most disastrous conflicts in which Britain has ever fought. There was little experience in the cabinet of such weighty matters. Furthermore, the military leaders in place at the time – men such as Lord Fitzroy Somerset, 1st Baron Raglan (1788-1855), who was Commander-in-Chief of the British Crimean Expeditionary Forces and James Brudenell, seventh Earl of Cardigan (1797-1868), famously the leader of the Charge of the Light Brigade during the war – were lacking in experience. They are not remembered for their strategic vision or their success in battle; if they are remembered at all, it is for their incompetence.

The British and French forces could not directly attack Sebastopol because of the impressive fortifications the Russians had installed. They decided, therefore, to make landfall to the south of the port. This was achieved in September 1854. The Allied forces numbered 56,000. Facing them were 80,000 Russian troops. On 20 September, the Allies defeated a Russian force at Alma but the French were reluctant to pursue the advantage they had gained and the operation came to nothing. Unfortunately, matters were not proceeding as well at sea and the Russians sank seven Allied vessels. This also made it impossible to proceed at that time. By October, however, it appeared that the Allies were on the verge of taking Sebastopol. The Russians responded by launching two attacks. The first, at Balaclava, on 25 October, is famous for the attack on the

Russian lines by the British Heavy and Light Brigades of Cavalry that became the subject of the celebrated poem by Lord Tennyson, 'The Charge of the Light Brigade', with its famous refrain:

'Cannon to right of them,
Cannon to left of them,
Cannon behind them
Volleyed and thundered;
Stormed at with shot and shell,
While horse and hero fell.
They that had fought so well
Came through the jaws of Death,
Back from the mouth of hell,
All that was left of them,
Left of six hundred.'

Russia sent reinforcements, raising their troop numbers to 120,000 a few weeks later. The Allies, too, had bolstered their strength with the addition of 11,000 Turkish troops. At the Battle of Inkerman on 5 November, 2,573 British troops lost their lives compared to only 143 French but the Russians lost many more. Unfortunately, however, the Allies next had to contend with an even more difficult enemy – the Russian winter. They were ill-prepared, lacking medicines, munitions and even food, as Parliament had cut expenditure on many supplies. Diseases such as cholera and dysentery were prevalent and things looked very bad for the Allies.

The Crimean War is famous for many things, few of them good, but perhaps the most significant figure to emerge from it was a nurse who would become one of the most celebrated individuals of the nineteenth century – Florence Nightingale (1820-1910). In October 1854, after persuading Sidney Herbert (1810-61), Secretary of State for War in Aberdeen's cabinet, she was sent along with 38 other volunteer nurses, trained by her, and 15 Catholic nuns, to Selimiye Barracks in Scutari (modern-day Üsküdar) near Istanbul. British wounded were transported there in a long and arduous journey. She and her team were appalled by the conditions and apparent indifference of officialdom to the plight of the injured soldiers. There were insufficient medicines and scant regard for hygiene and cleanliness which meant that deadly infections were rife, many of them proving fatal.

Nightingale sent a desperate letter to the *Times* back in London, urging the government to do something to improve the conditions in which medical staff were being forced to work. The government responded by commissioning Isambard Kingdom Brunel to design a prefabricated hospital that could be made in Britain and shipped to Turkey. Renkioi hospital was created, a facility in which the death rate was reduced by 90 per cent. Meanwhile, Nightingale herself further reduced the death rate by introducing handwashing and other hygiene measures. She would inspect the wards at night carrying a lamp, a practice that resulted in her being dubbed 'the lady with the lamp'. The *Times* described her as:

'...a "ministering angel" without any exaggeration in these hospitals, and as her slender form glides quietly along each corridor, every poor fellow's face softens with gratitude at the sight of her. When all the medical officers have retired for the night and silence and darkness have settled down upon those miles of prostrate sick, she may be observed alone, with a little lamp in her hand, making her solitary rounds.'

In 1855, the Nightingale Fund for the training of nurses was established. With £45,000 raised by the fund, she founded the Nightingale Training School – now the Florence Nightingale School of Nursing and Midwifery – at St Thomas' Hospital in London. She lived until the age of 90 and, in 1907, became the first woman to receive the Order of Merit.

The Crimean War also created something that would remain with us to this day – investigative journalism. The *Times* correspondent, William Howard Russell (1820-1907) provided candid commentary on the war and the dreadful conditions being endured which for the first time was able to be read just days after the events described, due to the telegraph that linked the Crimea to Britain. No longer could war be seen as a noble pursuit; instead it was described in all its horror by Russell. This resulted in outrage from the British public and outright hostility to a conflict that many believed should not have been fought. An anti-war movement emerged, led by John Bright and Richard Cobden, founders also of the Anti-Corn Law League and free-trade champions. They were berated in the press but remained firm in their belief that too many were dying in the war and that it was wrong to fight on the side of Turkey, a country they described as corrupt and backward. Although ultimately unsuccessful, Bright delivered one of the century's greatest and most eloquent speeches in Parliament in February 1855, in which he said:

'The angel of death has been abroad throughout the land; you may almost hear the beating of his wings. There is no one, as when the first-born were slain of old, to sprinkle with blood the lintel and the two sideposts of our doors, that he may spare and pass on; he takes his victims from the castle of the noble, the mansion of the wealthy, and the cottage of the poor and the lowly, and it is on behalf of all these classes that I make this solemn appeal. I tell the noble Lord, that if he be ready honestly and frankly to endeavour, by the negotiations to be opened at Vienna, to put an end to this war, no word of mine, no vote of mine, will be given to shake his power for one single moment, or to change his position in this House.'

Nevertheless, the great majority of people and newspapers fully supported the war and before long, they were sensing victory. Sebastopol fell to the Allies in September 1855 and, in the ensuing Treaty of Paris of 1856, Turkish independence was guaranteed. Russia agreed not to establish any bases on the Black Sea coast, rendering its naval threat to the Ottoman Empire redundant.

The war had cost Britain dear. 24,000 British soldiers lost their lives but there was also a heavy financial cost. British military spending rocketed from £15.3 million in 1853 to £27.5 million in 1855. And for the remainder of the nineteenth century it amounted to more than £20 million a year. Gladstone raised taxes to pay for it, avoiding the nightmare of increased borrowing and the burden of those debts falling on future generations.

Around this time, new weaponry was being developed that would change the nature of warfare forever. The Armstrong gun, for instance, a rifled breech-loading field gun, was created in the mid-1850s by the industrialist, scientist and inventor, Sir William Armstrong (1810-1900), at his factory on Tyneside. Three years later, he gave the patent to the government. A forerunner of the machine gun and heavy shelling, it would help to change the nature of warfare. There were other developments, such as the building of the first armoured British ship, HMS *Warrior*, acknowledged to be the prototype of the modern battleship.

The political fall-out from the disastrous handling of the war was considerable. On the day that a Radical MP announced that he was seeking a committee of enquiry into the conduct of the war, Lord John Russell resigned. This was followed by the resignation of the Aberdeen government on 29 January 1855, the day that the Protectionists and the radicals joined forces in support of the establishment of the committee of enquiry.

The Return of Palmerston

The choice of the next Prime Minister fell to the queen and Prince Albert, and the last person they wanted in 10 Downing Street was Palmerston. Her first choice, Earl of Derby, gave up when Palmerston and Gladstone refused to join a government that would be dominated by Tories. When her next choice, Lord John Russell, was similarly unable to form a government, she had no option but to turn to the 72-year-old Palmerston. He succeeded in forming a government, but following his blocking of the enquiry into the war, the leading Peelites in his government – Gladstone, Herbert and Sir James Graham (1792-1861) – resigned. The government that Palmerston led was now entirely Whig-

Liberal. It was not thought that he would be in power for very long, but he confounded his many critics by remaining in office – apart from a brief hiatus from February 1858 to June 1859 – until his death in 1865. He may have had critics, but he was extremely popular in the country, not least because he cultivated a strong relationship with the press and paid close attention to the views of the electorate. He also benefited from the comparatively peaceful and stable times during which he held the highest office.

Reform continued under his premiership. Newspapers once again prospered from the abolition of stamp duty; British companies were permitted to assume limited liability status which enabled them to issue shares without shareholders being held responsible for losses or debts incurred; the Metropolitan Board of Works was created to coordinate work that needed to be carried out to improve London's infrastructure; and the Obscene Publications Act of 1857 made it illegal to publish literature that could be deemed obscene. The 1857 Matrimonial Causes Act reformed the law on divorce, moving cases from ecclesiastical courts to civil courts and basing marriage on a contract basis rather than sacrament. Divorce was available previously only to those who could afford to sue for an annulment or those who could promote a private bill in Parliament. Now it was made more accessible. However, as we have seen, it remained easier for men to petition for divorce than for women. Gladstone, in particular, loathed this piece of legislation because it brought divorce within the reach of every class of person.

Early in the government's tenure, however, matters abroad took on more importance. News arrived in London of the seizure by the Chinese at Canton of a small British cargo ship, the *Arrow*. The vessel had previously been used for piracy and had been seized and resold by the Chinese. It was reregistered as a British ship and flew the British flag, although its registration had expired when it was seized once again. When demands for the immediate release of the crew and an apology for pulling down the British flag were ignored, the British Consul in Hong Kong, Sir Harry Smith Parkes (1828-1885), reported the incident to the Governor of Hong Kong, Sir John Bowring (1792-1872), presenting it as an insult to Britain. Bowring, seeing an opportunity to gain free access to the port of Canton, guaranteed in the Treaty of Nanking, but so far denied, ordered that Canton be bombarded, and guns of the Royal Navy opened fire on 28 December 1856. News of the incident arrived in London in February and the action of the governor was endorsed by Palmerston. Parliament did not support him, however, and a censure motion promoted by Richard Cobden passed by 263 votes to 247 in the Commons. Palmerston took the matter to the country and won a majority of 85 seats.

Palmerston's foreign policy was supported across the

country and several of his most vocal critics – including Richard Cobden and John Bright – lost their seats in the election. But, there was trouble ahead for him. In January 1858, an attempt was made in Paris on the life of the French Emperor Napoleon III. The failed assassin was an Italian revolutionary, Felice Orsini (1819-58), who was arrested following the incident and executed. When it was discovered that the explosives had been made in Britain, Napoleon demanded that the British government ensured that such a thing would never happen again. Palmerston did as he was asked and legislation was introduced to deal with such matters. But it was voted down by the Tories, who had united with the Peelites and the radicals on the vote in order to bring down the government. The Earl of Derby became Prime Minister and his government's brief period in power brought some domestic legislation – the property qualification for MPs was abolished and Jews were allowed to become MPs – but the administration fell when a relatively inconsequential measure on parliamentary reform, introduced by Disraeli, was rejected.

The March 1859 election saw the Conservatives winning 298 seats, a gain of 34 but Palmerston's Whigs returned to power. A momentous meeting with Peelites, radicals, Liberals and Whigs at Willis's tea rooms in June 1859 put him in a good position, and he and Russell agreed to work together for the good of the country while

Gladstone decided to change allegiance from the Tories to the Liberals, now officially known as the Liberal Party. Palmerston's government put Russell in the Foreign Office and Gladstone returned as Chancellor. It could be described as a Liberal government, and the Peelites also became part of the Liberal Party.

The Indian Mutiny

By 1857, the East India Company army was made up of around 50,000 British troops and about 300,000 sepoys, the lowest ranking local soldiers, who were mostly Muslim or Hindu. The Company tried to accommodate the requirements of these men. For example, Hindu troops did not have to serve overseas as their religion teaches that crossing the sea results in the loss of one's *varna*, or class status, caste being of great importance to Hindus. Hindu troops were also permitted to observe their festivals and celebrations.

There were many complaints from the troops, however. They were expected to serve in places such as Burma and the extra pay that had once been given them for such service was no longer available. In July 1856, the Governor-General of India, the Marquess of Dalhousie (1812-60) introduced the General Service Enlistment Act. This act required new recruits to accept a commitment to general service which meant serving abroad. Existing troops feared that this would soon be extended to them. There was also the issue of promotion. Increasingly, officers were of European extraction and it was difficult for an Indian soldier to progress through the ranks and improve his prospects.

The ammunition for the new Enfield P-53 rifle was another issue that contributed to the disquiet in the ranks. These used paper cartridges that were coated in grease. Before inserting the cartridge in his rifle, a sepoy had to bite open the paper enveloping the cartridge in order to release the powder. A rumour grew that the grease used was derived from cows, which made it offensive to Hindus who believed that the cow was sacred, and pigs which rendered it unclean for Muslims. The British immediately stopped production of the cartridges when they realised how great the problem was. An order went out that the sepoys could grease them instead, using whatever material they chose. Furthermore, they could be opened by hand instead of biting. The sepoys divined from this that the rumour must have been true and that animal fat had been used.

At the same time, there was considerable unrest amongst the general population. Centuries of tradition had been overturned by the introduction of the Doctrine of Lapse, a policy that dictated that if a ruler of a princely state (the small states that served as vassal states to Britain in India) died without a male heir, the state's princely status would be abolished and it would be annexed by the British Empire. Previously, a sovereign without an heir had the right to appoint a successor of his choice. Punitive land taxes were another factor and the abolition of some Hindu practices, such as *sati* in which a widow immolated herself on her husband's funeral pyre. Indians claimed that the British were interfering with their religious practices and beliefs.

The Indian Mutiny, or Great Rebellion, as it is sometimes called, began on 10 May 1857, when sepoys based at Meerut, 35 miles northeast of Delhi, mutinied, killing every European they encountered. Civilians began to join their ranks as they made for Delhi. At Delhi Fort they met with Bahadur Shah II (r. 1837-57), the Mughal emperor, and requested that he led the rebellion. Bahadur agreed only reluctantly but gave his public support to the uprising. Quickly spreading across North India, the revolt was joined by many leaders of the various royal families.

Initially, the British were slow to react, but large numbers of troops had soon been brought in, including regiments from the Crimean War and regiments *en route* for China. They laid siege to Delhi from 1 July until 31 August, at which point there was street-fighting between the British and the Indians. The city was retaken for the empire, but the retribution was terrible. An anonymous letter about the British capture of Delhi was published in the *Bombay Telegraph* in September 1857:

'All the city people found within the walls when our troops entered were bayoneted on the spot; and the number was considerable, as you may suppose, when I tell you that in some houses forty and fifty people were hiding. These were not mutineers, but residents of the city, who trusted to our well-known mild rule for pardon. I am glad to say they were disappointed.'

At Kanpur 120 British women and children were massacred by the sepoys. The horror of this incident was described by an observer in a book entitled *Cawnpore*, written eight years after the mutiny:

'The bodies... were dragged out, most of them by the hair of the head. Those who had clothes worth taking were stripped. Some of the women were alive. I cannot say how many... They prayed for the sake of God that an end might be put to their sufferings... Three boys were alive. They were fair children. The eldest, I think, must have been six or seven, and the youngest five years. They were running round the well (where else could they go to?) and there was none to save them. No: none said a word or tried to save them.'

At Lucknow there was a prolonged defence of the Residency – the British political office of the city – that lasted from June until November 1857. The rebellion was over shortly after that, although some guerrilla fighting continued until the first months of 1859.

Bahadur Shah proved to be the last Mughal emperor. He was sent into exile at Rangoon (now Yangon) in Burma where he died in 1862. The most important outcome of the Indian Rebellion of 1857, however, was the end of the East India Company after two and a half centuries. The British government withdrew the Company's right to rule India in November 1858 and Queen Victoria's pronouncement of this was read out at every station in India. The Governor-General was now the queen's representative in India and the British bent over backwards to reassure the Indians. It was guaranteed that all the treaties that the Company had made with native princes would be honoured; there would be no more annexations; there would be a general amnesty for all rebels apart from those who had been involved in the murder of Europeans; all religions would be tolerated and ancient Indian customs would be respected. India became part of the British Empire with Queen Victoria assuming the title 'Empress of India' in 1876.

Literature in the 1850s

Of huge importance to the world of books was the Public Libraries Act of 1850 that gave local boroughs the right to establish free public lending libraries. Indeed, workers now had free time, as a result of the reforms that had been passed by Parliament in such legislation as the Factory Act of 1833.

Many of the Victorian middle class were concerned that they would spend this time badly and campaigners sought to encourage workers to devote their free time to morally uplifting pursuits such as reading. An earlier bill had failed but had encouraged MPs to introduce the Museums Act of 1845 which empowered boroughs of a certain size to raise money for the establishment of museums. Public libraries followed even though some objected to the extra tax and others worried that libraries would become places where social unrest could be encouraged. Nonetheless, the thousands of libraries that we have today owe their existence to this legislation.

The literary critiques of British society that had begun to appear in the 1840s, were still being written during the following decade. Dickens added to his considerable output at the very start of the decade with his eighth work of fiction, *David Copperfield*, which many considered to be highly autobiographical. As in several of his other works, he highlights examples of child exploitation and cruelty, and a number of his most famous characters appear, including Wilkins Micawber and Uriah Heep. It appeared in 19 monthly episodes in Dickens's periodical, *Household Words*, from May 1849 to November 1850, before being published in book form in the month in which the last episode appeared. He continued to provide scathing social commentary in his satire of the English judicial system, *Bleak House* (1853) and in *Hard Times* (1854) and

Little Dorrit (1856). Also originally serialised in Dickens's periodical, *Household Words*, Elizabeth Gaskell's novel *Cranford* (1853) was an affectionate portrait of the people and the changing customs and habits of the small town of the title. She went on to examine the plight of factory workers in *North and South* (1855) while Charles Kingsley's *Alton Locke* (1850) displayed sympathy with the Chartist movement, with which he had himself been involved in the 1840s. Kingsley also wrote the historical novels *Hypatia* (1853) and *Westward Ho!* (1855), in the latter of which he narrates the adventures of Elizabethan corsair, Amyas Preston (Amyas Leigh in the novel). William Thackeray was less fascinated by the plight of the working man and more interested in social climbing and snobbery. His novel, *The Newcomes*, published in 1855, followed the fortunes of an 'arriviste' respectable, extended middle-class family of the 1830s and 1840s.

Also in 1855, Anthony Trollope (1815-1882) launched his Chronicles of Barsetshire series of six novels with *The Warden*, a tale of English ecclesiastical life featuring a kindly clergyman who becomes involved in a scandal when he is accused of financial impropriety. The second novel in the series, *Barchester Towers* followed two years later. A new generation of writers was beginning to emerge by the end of the decade. The master of mystery, Wilkie Collins (1824-89), published his acclaimed *The Woman in White* in 1859, and George Meredith (1828-1909) who would be nominated for the Nobel Prize in Literature no fewer than seven times, published *The Ordeal of Richard Feverel*, the story of a man's efforts to win freedom from his domineering father and the failure of education to dull human passions.

At that time, novels were often published in serial form in newspapers and periodicals before they appeared in book form. This was true of Dickens, Collins, Thackeray and Trollope. Dickens, in fact, founded and edited a weekly magazine entitled *All the Year Round*, that appeared between 1859 and 1895. It followed his previous publishing effort, *Household Words*. Direct competition to Dickens's publication was provided by *The Cornhill*, edited by Thackeray. Reading material for most people, however, consisted of what were known as 'penny dreadfuls', cheap, sensational serial literature, published in weekly parts and costing a penny. The stories were of detectives, criminals and supernatural beings. Many other periodicals catered for those not seeking great literature.

In 1859, a woman named Mary Ann Evans (1819-80) published a novel, *Adam Bede*. Born in the Midlands, she had been very well educated for a girl of her time. She spoke French, German and Italian and had studied science, philosophy and religion. But, in her twenties, she rejected religion. Moving to London in 1851, she became assistant editor of the radical left-wing journal, *The Westminster Review*, a highly unusual position for a woman to hold. From 1853, she lived with the writer and critic, George Henry

Lewes (1817-78), even though he was already married. For her first novel, Evans adopted the *nom de plume* George Eliot and under this sobriquet, she would go on to write a number of other nineteenth-century classics that often featured social outsiders and the persecution that can occur in small towns. She was a realist who brought sophisticated character portraits and profound psychological insight to her work.

Henry Mayhew (1812–1887) was an interesting character who dipped a toe into various strands of literature. He was a co-founder and co-editor of the humorous satirical magazine, *Punch*, which had first been published in 1841 and continued until its last issue in 2002, with only a slight hiatus between 1992 and 1996. Mayhew also wrote for the early issues of *The Illustrated London News*. He is best remembered, however, for *London Labour and London Poor*, a shocking description of the plight of the capital's disadvantaged that had first appeared in the *Morning Chronicle* but was published in three volumes in 1851. Based on interviews with ordinary working people, it exposed the dreadful conditions being endured by many in the greatest city in the world. London may, indeed, have been the world's richest city but those who ran it had failed to respond to the massive increase in population in the first decades of the century. It was polluted by fog and infested with fever. Its population had more than doubled while public services had remained virtually unaltered.

New in the 1850s

The red pillar post box that became so characteristic of Britain arrived in 1852 when the first examples were erected in Guernsey. Early examples in Britain would be green, however. In 1857, wall boxes at the sides of roads appeared, but mainland Britain's first pillar box was installed in 1856 at Botchergate, a street in Carlisle. An ornate pillar box, intended for use in London and other cities was designed in 1856 by the artist and administrator, Richard Redgrave (1804-88), inspector-general for art at the Department of Science and Art, and this design was upgraded in 1859. It became the very first National Standard pillar box. Between 1866 and 1879, the Penfold pillar box, designed by surveyor and architect, John Penfold (1828-1909), would become the standard design and pillar boxes began to be painted red.

The railways continued to grow and had reached the outskirts of built-up London by the 1850s. In 1846, the standard railway gauge of 4 feet 8½ inches was stipulated by Act of Parliament. Some railway companies pressed ahead with development using the old, broad gauge, however. The Great Western Railway used it to push into the Midlands, reaching Birmingham in 1852, and Wolverhampton in 1854. Some used mixed gauge so that trains of either gauge could run, and it would take until 1876 to dispense with the final piece of broad gauge in Britain. Meanwhile, railway structures were also built, one of the most famous being the Britannia Bridge across the Menai Strait, opened in 1850 and linking the island of Anglesey with the Welsh mainland. Designed by Robert Stephenson, it was a tubular bridge of wrought-iron rectangular box-section spans.

The public flushing toilet first made an appearance at the Great Exhibition in Hyde Park where George Jennings (1810-82), a water closet manufacturer based at Parkstone Pottery in Poole, installed what he called his Monkey Closets in the Retiring Rooms. These were the first public pay toilets and 827,280 visitors paid one penny to use them. It was a good deal – customers were allowed to use the toilet but also received a towel, a comb and a shoe shine. Thus, the euphemism, to 'spend a penny' entered the English language. Jennings also opened the first underground toilet at the Royal Exchange in 1854. His 1852 patent improved the construction of the water closet, the pan and trap being constructed in one piece, which meant that there was always a small quantity of water retained in the pan. By the end of the decade, most new middle-class homes had a water closet.

In the world of children's health there was a significant development with the founding of the first hospital in England specifically for children. Great Ormond Street Hospital, founded in 1852, was the result of a long campaign by Dr Charles West (1816-98). Initially, it had a mere ten beds but, through the patronage of Queen Victoria and the fundraising of Charles Dickens, would become one of the world's leading children's hospitals.

About this time, a number of great public buildings were constructed around Britain. In Bradford, the neo-classical St George's Hall was financed by a joint-stock company and incorporated a restaurant and a concert hall that boasted a splendid organ. The Manchester Free Trade Hall was financed by public subscription, the money being raised between 1853 and 1856. It became the home of the Hallé Orchestra, one of the first orchestras to be established outside the capital. The most splendid of all was Leeds Town Hall, built between 1853 and 1858, and financed by joint stock and the local council. It was opened by Queen Victoria and Prince Albert.

4

The 1860s:
The Widow of Windsor

The Death of the Prince Consort

On 14 December 1861, the country was shocked by the death of the Prince Consort, Prince Albert. He had become very ill in August 1859 with stomach cramps, but in spite of his continuing discomfort, in March 1861 he assumed his wife's duties during the mourning period following the death of her mother, the Duchess of Kent. The last event he attended in this capacity was the opening of the Royal Horticultural Gardens on 5 June. In August, he accompanied the Queen to the Curragh camp in Ireland where their son, the Prince of Wales, was billeted. By November, the royal couple were at Windsor and the Prince of Wales had returned to his studies at Cambridge. There was bad news, however. Two of Albert's young cousins, 24-year-old King Pedro V of Portugal (r. 1853-61) and his 15-year-old brother Prince

Ferdinand (1846-61) had died of typhoid within days of each other. To make matters worse, rumours reached Victoria and Albert that the Prince of Wales was still involved with the actress Nellie Clifden whom he had met at a party in England and again at the Curragh camp. The royal couple were distressed at this news, realising the scandal that could result. Although ailing, and now suffering from pain in his back and legs, Albert travelled to Cambridge to speak to his son on 25 November. By this time, he was very ill and on 9 December, he was diagnosed with typhoid fever – a diagnosis questioned by modern doctors. Five days later he died at Windsor Castle, aged 42, surrounded by his wife and five of their nine children.

Prince Albert had, in later years, become closer to Palmerston, especially during his premiership when he was less inclined to employ the gunboat diplomacy of his time as Foreign Secretary. Albert was a moderate in his approach to foreign policy and was an exemplar of his age, high-minded and earnest. Above all, he was an exceptional family man. It is, of course, difficult to say what would have happened had he lived. As the century progressed, would this German prince have had an influence on the way German unification happened and on other matters? It is, of course, impossible to say. It is certainly true, however, that there was a deep sadness at his death and Queen Victoria was, naturally, devastated by it. She believed that the Prince of Wales's philandering – 'that dreadful business', as she described it – was the cause of her husband's death. Now, she began to dress in black, the colour she wore for the rest of her life, and she withdrew from public life for the next ten years. She became known as the 'widow of Windsor' and put on a great deal of weight. It is said that, until her death, every night she had her maids lay out Prince Albert's clothes for the next day and the water in the basin in his room was changed every day.

Her absence from the public gaze encouraged republican tendencies in Britain. She secluded herself in Windsor Castle, at Balmoral – the beloved private estate she and Albert had bought in 1851 – or at Osborne House on the Isle of Wight. In 1864 a notice was pinned to the railings at Buckingham Palace by a protester that read: '…these premises to be let or sold in consequence of the late occupant's declining business.' During the years following her husband's death, Queen Victoria formed a close relationship with one of her outdoor servants at Balmoral. John Brown (1826-83) was born at Crathie, near the estate and worked as a ghillie on the estate but salacious rumours soon started spreading about the relationship. Some suggested that the two had secretly married and people gave the queen the nickname 'Mrs Brown'. When Brown died, Victoria wrote in a letter:

'Perhaps never in history was there so strong and true an attachment, so warm and loving a friendship between the sovereign and servant… Strength of character as well as power of frame – the most fearless uprightness, kindness, sense of justice, honesty, independence and unselfishness combined with a tender, warm heart... made him one of the most remarkable men. The Queen feels that life for the second time is become most trying and sad to bear deprived of all she so needs... the blow has fallen too heavily not to be very heavily felt...'

More Reform

Another death four years later stunned the nation. The Prime Minister, Lord Palmerston caught a chill on 12 October 1865. It developed into a fever but then he seemed to rally. On 17 October, however, his condition deteriorated and he passed away the following day. An apocryphal version of his death suggests that, when his doctor informed him that he was going to die, he answered, 'Die, my dear doctor? That is the last thing I shall do.' His last words were, in fact, to do with diplomatic treaties – 'That's Article 98: now go on to the next.'

In his last spell in power, some important legislation was passed. In 1861, the Offences Against the Person Act brought together a number of statutes relating to the committing of direct physical harm to another person or force being applied to someone else. The aim of the Act was to simplify and codify the law. Although amended subsequently, it remains the foundation for the prosecution of personal injury – short of murder – in English and Welsh courts. In 1862, the Companies Act was passed, providing the basis for modern company law.

One of Palmerston's most intractable problems during this last premiership was his relationship with his Chancellor of the Exchequer, William Gladstone. A member of the Cabinet told the MP Sir William Gregory (1816-92) how Cabinet meetings sometimes went:

'...at the beginning of each session and after each holiday, Mr Gladstone used to come in charged to the muzzle with all sorts of schemes of all sorts of reforms which were absolutely necessary in his opinion to be immediately undertaken. Palmerston used to look fixedly at the paper before him, saying nothing until there was a lull in Gladstone's outpouring. He then rapped the table and said cheerfully: "Now, my Lords and gentlemen, let us go to business"'

Indeed, Palmerston was convinced that, when he was gone, Gladstone would wreck the Liberal Party.

On another occasion, when, in May 1864, the MP Edward Baines (1800-90) was introducing a Reform Bill in the House of Commons, Palmerston forbade Gladstone from committing the government to support of the bill. In his speech, Gladstone insisted that he could not see why any man should not have the vote unless he was mentally incapacitated. However, he went on, this would not arrive unless the working class demonstrated that it was interested in reform. For Palmerston, this was little short of encouraging the working class to agitate for reform. He angrily told Gladstone: 'What every Man and Woman, too, have a Right to, is to be well governed and under just laws, and they who propose a change ought to shew that the present organization does not accomplish those objects.'

When France and Sardinia went to war with the Austrian Empire in Italy in 1859, there was concern in Britain that a belligerent France might also cross the Channel and invade Britain. The Royal Commission on the Defence of the United Kingdom, convened by Palmerston, recommended a massive construction programme of defensive fortifications on the coast to protect the Royal Navy and British ports. The Prime Minister was in full agreement with the Commission but Gladstone objected vehemently to the huge cost that would be incurred and threatened to resign. In fact, Palmerston told someone that he had received so many resignation letters from his Chancellor that he feared they would set fire to his chimney.

In July 1865, not long before Palmerston died, a general election was held in which his Liberal Party increased its already large majority over the Earl of Derby's Conservative Party to more than 80. Before

Parliament assembled, however, Palmerston was dead. Instead of sending for a younger man such as Gladstone, Queen Victoria summoned Russell to the palace. He had been elevated to the peerage in 1861 and sat in the House of Lords for the rest of his political career. The government he formed was short-lived, lasting a mere nine months, and most of the members of Palmerston's government remained in their posts, including Gladstone as Chancellor. This short period was dominated by the issue of reform, the extension of the franchise to more urban skilled workers. Proposals featured the lowering of the franchise qualification to give the vote to adult males who paid £7 or more in rent. Gladstone introduced the new reform bill in April 1866 but it split the Liberal Party – the split engineered by Disraeli – and the bill was defeated. Russell's government resigned, to be replaced by a Tory minority administration, led by the Earl of Derby, with Benjamin Disraeli leading the government in the Commons. Russell, after a glorious career in which he was Prime Minister twice, Foreign Secretary twice, Home Secretary and Secretary of State for War and the Colonies, never held public office again and it was up to Gladstone to fly the flag of Liberalism. The era of Gladstone and Disraeli had arrived, in which these two politicians would dominate British politics.

Disraeli Takes Office

Disraeli was determined to prove to the electorate that the Conservatives were a viable governing party and, to that end, he aimed to get some legislation through Parliament. Reform remained firmly on the agenda, particularly after riots in support of it in Hyde Park in the summer of 1866, and demonstrations led by radicals such as John Bright. It was not the upsurge of indignation that had gripped the nation in previous decades, but it kept the issue uppermost in the minds of the politicians and made them mindful about the possibility of unrest on a larger scale. Disraeli created a reform bill, therefore, that he hoped to be able to sell to Conservative backbenchers and Liberals alike. Although he had initially intended the bill to be very much more moderate than Gladstone's of the previous year, in the months after he introduced it in March 1867, he adopted a great many amendments that served to make it even more radical than the one introduced by his great rival. Supported by all Tories who wished to retain power, having been out of office for so long, as well as enough Liberals, the bill passed through Parliament. It was a brilliant parliamentary performance by Disraeli and enabled him to succeed Derby as leader of the Conservative Party and Prime Minister when the latter retired in February 1868. It was first blood to Disraeli in his rivalry with Gladstone.

There may have been several reasons why Disraeli and

a Conservative government introduced such a radical bill. The first reason was, of course, to beat Gladstone and the Liberals. But it also should be remembered that the Conservatives had not won a majority in the Commons since the Peelite split 20 years previously. In fact, they had lost five successive general elections. Therefore, it can reasonably be asked, what did they have to lose? And there was a chance, as Disraeli and a number of his party believed, that by extending the franchise to urban workers, they might find new followers and new votes. The 1867 Representation of the People Act, as it was rather grandly known, extended the vote to all rate-paying male householders who had lived at their address for at least a year and to male lodgers paying rent of at least £10 a year who had been resident there for at least a year. In county seats, the franchise was extended to include males who occupied land worth at least £12 a year or who owned land that was worth at least £5. This was £14 in Scotland.

There were also changes to parliamentary seats, disenfranchising a number that returned two MPs and five which returned one MP. Thirty-five boroughs that had previously returned two members had their representation reduced to one. Therefore, 52 of the smaller boroughs lost representation entirely and 19 new ones replaced them. There were a number of other changes including some to county seats. Scotland and Wales did not see a great deal of change, however. The Act brought almost a million new voters in England and Wales, an increase in the electorate of 88 per cent; in Scotland, there was an increase in the electorate of 119 per cent; but in Ireland, the increase was a mere 8 per cent. However, this meant that one in three adult males now had the vote in England, Wales and Scotland, while in Ireland that figure was one in six. There were still anomalies – a man owning property in a number of different constituencies could vote in each of those places and there were even more university seats. However, it could be described as pretty radical, creating for the first time a mass, working-class electorate in the towns and cities of Britain.

At the same time, it might be argued that Disraeli was only introducing such legislation for the benefit of his party. Many of the small boroughs whose representation he abolished were resolutely Whig or Liberal while the large cities – especially London – were poorly represented. London had only slightly more than twenty MPs, four of those coming from the City, voted for by the wealthy business elite who worked in that particular area. The East End had only four MPs. The Act was designed to prohibit the Liberals or the radicals from gaining any more seats and, to that end, Disraeli did a brilliant job.

It is worthy of note that as the 1867 bill was being debated, the great philosopher John Stuart Mill, a Liberal MP, brought forward a bill to gain the vote for women. The measure was defeated by 196 votes to 73 and it would not be until February 1918 that this would finally come to pass. But even then it was granted only to women over the age of 30 who met minimum property requirements.

Other Significant Events of the 1860s

Friendly societies and insurance companies had opened in the 1850s – the Royal Liver in 1850, the Prudential in 1854. They would help to lessen the burden of the working class under constant threat of unemployment, injury and the inability to pay for funerals. Saving and thrift became more common. To help in this area, in 1861, Palmerston's government launched the Post Office Savings Bank, the first postal savings system anywhere in the world. It began in two small rooms within the headquarters of the GPO (General Post Office) in St Martin's-le-Grand in London. By 1863, however, it had grown so much that it occupied a warehouse at St Paul's Churchyard. The stated aim of the bank was to enable ordinary working people 'to provide for themselves against adversity and ill-health'. It was attractive because it was backed by the government. Of course, it also benefited the government to have access to all that money and it was used by the Chancellor, Gladstone, to offset against public spending. It was the beginning of a mechanism that would enable the government to raise funds by issuing savings certificates during the two World Wars and to launch Premium Bonds in 1956. The bank, today called National Savings & Investments, now handles around £150 billion in savings.

London's rapidly growing population in the nineteenth century had brought problems in many areas of life. Getting around the capital was one of them. The great numbers of people arriving each day for work or just a visit were becoming overwhelming and every day the streets were clogged up with carts, carriages, cabs and omnibuses. The railway had come into the metropolis and by 1850 there were seven railway termini across it. The notion of having an underground railway system that would link all of these and remove some of the traffic from London's congested streets had first been floated in the 1830s by the Solicitor to the City of London and social reformer, Charles Pearson (1793-1862). He proposed a central railway station for the City that would make it possible for commuters to travel to the City from further away. After the rejection of this plan, he proposed an underground railway and, in 1852, contributed towards the establishment of the City Terminus Company that was created to build a railway underground from Farringdon to King's Cross. There was little interest from railway companies, however. Then, in 1854, the Metropolitan Railway was given permission to build an underground line. But, against the background of the Crimean War, it struggled to raise the £1 million required. It was not, therefore, until 1860 that work started on the railway. It opened on 10 January 1863, and consisted of steam locomotives pulling open carriages through the tunnels. On its first day, it was used by 38,000 people. And in the first year of service, it carried 9.5 million passengers.

The decade saw many more innovations. The Football Association, the world's first such organisation, met for the first time on 26 October 1863 at the Freemasons' Tavern on Great Queen Street in London's Covent Garden area. Until then, there had been no generally accepted set of rules for football, although it had been played for centuries. Public schools each had their own set of rules and Cambridge University had published a set of rules in 1848, known as the Cambridge Rules. In the north of England, however, football was played to the Sheffield Rules. The October 1863 meeting of eleven London football clubs and representatives from the schools was to agree on one set of rules. The driving force behind all this was Ebenezer Cobb Morley (1831-1924), captain of the Barnes football team. He wrote to *Bell's Life* newspaper proposing that there should be one organisation controlling football which led to the meeting at the Freemasons' Tavern and the creation of the Football Association. Morley became the FA's first secretary and drafted the laws of the game at his home in Barnes. He also took part in the first ever match under the new rules.

Golf came to the fore in October 1860 when the very first British Open Championship was staged at the Prestwick Golf Club in Scotland. The first prize – a red leather belt with a silver buckle – was won by Scottish golfer, Willie Park Sr (1833-1903). Amongst other significant moments, Vice-Admiral Robert Fitzroy (1805-65) developed the first means of forecasting the weather and daily weather forecasts were published in the *Times* from 1861; also in 1861, Samuel Beeton (1830-77) and his wife Isabella published *Mrs Beeton's Book of Household Management*; the Scottish banker, Sir Thomas Sutherland (1834-1922), founded the Hong Kong and Shanghai Banking Corporation (HSBC) in Hong Kong in 1866; in 1865, former Methodist Reform Church minister William Booth (1829-1912) held the first meeting of the Salvation Army – known at the time as the East London Christian Mission; and the United Kingdom set the first numeric speed limit of 10 miles per hour in towns in the Locomotive Act of 1861.

Literature in the 1860s

Charles Dickens maintained his astonishing creative productivity as the 1860s began with his *bildungsroman*, *Great Expectations*, published in thirty-six weekly episodes in *All the Year Round*, a magazine part-owned by him, between December 1860 and August 1861. It also appeared in serial form in *Harper's Weekly* in America, for which Dickens was paid £1,000. It is estimated that *All the Year Round* sold 100,000 copies of the *Great Expectations* issues each week. Featuring the customary array of extraordinary characters, such as Miss Havisham, the convict Magwitch and John Wemmick who lives with his 'Aged Parent', it narrates the story of an orphan named Pip. It is particularly noted for its opening scene, set in a graveyard where the young Pip encounters the escaped convict, Abel Magwitch. In 1865, Dickens's last completed novel was published – *Our Mutual Friend* – in which he cleverly combines savage satire and social comment.

George Eliot's *The Mill on the Floss* of 1860 was originally published in three volumes by the Scottish publisher, William Blackwood (1776-1834). Covering a period of 10 to 15 years, it narrates the lives of Tom and Maggie Tulliver, a brother and sister who are growing up in the late 1820s and early 1830s at the fictional Dorlcote Mill on the River Floss in Lincolnshire. A year later, Eliot published *Silas Marner*, an outwardly simple tale of a linen weaver which deals with a range of issues, from religion to the growing industrialisation that was creating tensions in communities at the time.

First serialised in the *Cornhill Magazine*, Elizabeth Gaskell's 1866 novel, *Wives and Daughters*, tells the story of Molly Gibson, the only daughter of a widowed doctor living in a provincial English town in the 1830s. Mrs Gaskell died suddenly in 1865 with the novel not quite finished. It was completed by the English journalist and man of letters, Frederick Greenwood (1830-1909).

Anthony Trollope had, by the mid-1860s, reached a fairly senior position in the Post Office, although he had issues with Rowland Hill who was Chief Secretary to the Postmaster General. Trollope does take the credit, however, for introducing the pillar box to Britain's streets. He was also earning considerable amounts of money from his novels. He launched a new series in 1865 – the Palliser novels – six books about British and Irish politics of the time. The first of these, *Can You Forgive Her?* was serialised from 1864 to 1865. The second of Trollope's Palliser novels, *Phineas Finn*, followed in 1867-8.

Richard Doddridge Blackmore – RD Blackmore – became one of the most acclaimed authors of the second half of the nineteenth century. His novel *Lorna Doone: A Romance of Exmoor*, was published in 1869 and remains a favourite to this day. Set in the late seventeenth century, it is a romantic tale featuring a set of historical characters. Blackmore initially had trouble finding a publisher and it first appeared anonymously in an edition of only 500 copies. A year later, when it was issued in an inexpensive one-volume edition, it became a huge critical and financial success.

5

The 1870s:
Gladstone and Disraeli

Gladstone's Government

To the modern sensibility, William Ewart Gladstone appears not to have been the most likeable of men. His high-mindedness, a Christian approach to politics that seems to modern eyes hypocritical, and his perpetual political changes of mind and position seem calculated and devious. But, to the people of his age, the 'Grand Old Man', as he was popularly known, was a highly respected leader, perhaps the greatest statesman who had ever strode the British political stage. At any rate, his shadow hovered over the Liberal Party for many years after his eventual death in 1898.

He would be Prime Minister of Great Britain four times, encompassing a period of twelve years – from December 1868 to February 1874; from April 1880 to June 1885; from February 1886 to July 1886; and from

August 1892 to March 1894. Born of Scottish parents in Liverpool in 1809, he was the fourth son of a very successful merchant and slave trader who was made Baron of Fasque and Balfour in 1846. Educated at Eton and Christ Church, Oxford, William Gladstone was already a Tory at university where he established a reputation for oratory as President of the Oxford Union and he was first elected to Parliament in 1832 as MP for Newark. In 1840, he began the practice of walking the streets of London, trying to persuade prostitutes that he met to change their way of life. Much to the annoyance of his colleagues, he continued to do this even after he had become Prime Minister. He was vehemently opposed to Britain's participation in the Opium War of 1840 – describing it as 'a war more unjust in its origin, a war more calculated in its progress to cover this country with permanent disgrace' – and he was also extremely vocal about the trade in opium in which Britain was involved. He built up a substantial following while in opposition, becoming known as 'the people's William'.

His championing of a policy to disestablish the Church of Ireland won him a great deal of support from those of a leftist persuasion, both in the country and in the House of Commons. Naturally, it was a move supported wholeheartedly by Irish MPs, aware of the huge unpopularity of the Anglican Church amongst their constituents. The Whigs, with their commitment to religious toleration were in favour and Nonconformists, suspicious of any religion with an allegiance to the state, of course, supported it. Gladstone pushed through three resolutions on the disestablishment in Parliament and he found support amongst voters in the 1868 general election following his campaign for disestablishment. His Liberal Party won by 371 seats to 271. This election was distinguished by being the first in Britain in which more than a million votes were cast. It was almost three times the number cast in the previous election.

For this election victory, Gladstone could look to what he described as 'our three *corps d'armeé*... Scotch Presbyterians, English and Welsh non-conformity, and Irish Roman Catholics'. He recognised that his party was successful in the further reaches of the union, but not in England. In contrast, the Conservatives relied on votes from English constituencies. This was one of the reasons behind Gladstone's preoccupation with Irish issues and he resolved to bring peace to Ireland.

The Cabinet he formed took little notice of the Second Reform Act and the same type of aristocratic politicians as ever were appointed. It was made up of 15 ministers including a duke, the heir to a dukedom, and four earls. There were others, however, who did come from humbler backgrounds. The Chancellor of the Exchequer, for instance, was Robert Lowe (1811-92), a barrister, and a vehement opponent of reform. The President of the Poor

Law Board was George Goschen (1831-1907), the son of a Liverpool merchant. Meanwhile, the Radical, John Bright, became the first Nonconformist to be a member of a British cabinet.

One reason for Ireland being so high on Gladstone's governmental agenda was the formation in Dublin in 1858 of the Irish Republican Brotherhood, commonly known as the Fenians. Supported financially by Irish exiles on the east coast of America, they sought independence for Ireland and believed it could be achieved only by armed revolution. By the mid-1850s, they had signed up 50,000 members. They launched a terrorist campaign in Britain in September 1867, when a group of them freed two of their colleagues from a prison van in Manchester, murdering an unarmed police sergeant in the process. The IRB tried to free another Fenian in December when they blew out a wall of Clerkenwell prison, killing 12 people and injuring 120 more. Three of the participants in the Manchester action were arrested and executed in some of the last public hangings to be staged in Britain. The British public was outraged by these actions and the resulting hostility damaged efforts to obtain Home Rule or independence for Ireland. But Irish nationalism was bolstered by the emergence of a strong nationalist organisation and Gladstone became convinced that, if the Union was to be maintained, Ireland had to be pacified. Thus, the Act that disestablished the Irish Church was passed in 1869. It was an obvious step because Ireland at the time was almost 80 per cent Roman Catholic and removing state support for the Church dispensed with one of the major symbols of British domination of Ireland.

Another issue with which Gladstone had to deal was far more complex. Many Irish landlords were absentee – often English – and they treated their tenants callously. The Irish Land Act of 1870 restricted the powers of landlords to evict tenants and gave tenants other protections. Government loans were also to be made available to them to purchase their smallholdings. Landowners found ways round the Act, though, and it was far from effective. To make matters worse, the loans were not sufficient for the tenants to be able to purchase their farms. Things continued much as they always had, landlords able to do as they wished and tenants still aggrieved.

Education, Civil Service and Military Reform

Education also needed to be addressed. Surveys suggested that almost fifty per cent of children aged between five and thirteen were not receiving elementary education. Some insisted that education was essential if Britain was to do well in future wars, citing the North's defeat of the South in the American Civil War and Prussia's success in recent conflicts. In each case, it was claimed, the better educated army was victorious. Others maintained that education was necessary now that many working-class men had been given the vote in the 1867 Representation of the People Act. If they were to use their votes wisely, they would need education.

The education system of the time can safely be described as 'chaotic' and far from good enough for a nation that claimed to be the world's most advanced industrial society. At the time, there were two camps – one that wished churches to remain in control of elementary education and another that sought secular schools. These were represented by two organisations. The National Education Union championed the continuation of the existing church-controlled system, while the National Education League supported the idea of non-sectarian schools and universal education.

The Elementary Education Act of 1870 was navigated through Parliament by William Edward Forster (1818-86) and was known as 'Forster's Education Act'. It allowed for the setting up of local education authorities in England and Wales which had defined powers and elected members, and money was to be distributed by them in order to improve schools. By the end of the decade some 3,000 schools came under the umbrella of such authorities. Spending on education rose. In London, for example, £1.6 million was spent on education in 1870 which rose to £5.1 million by 1885. The act, although an important moment in educational history in Britain, did create problems for the government. Many Nonconformists were dissatisfied with it and it was limited, dealing only with elementary education. Nothing was done for secondary schooling.

Universities, too, were undergoing change. The 1871 University Test Act opened teaching posts to Nonconformists and Jews. However, women were still prevented from teaching at universities. The Civil Service was dealt with in an Order in Council of 1870, and the old system of appointment, open to corruption and favouritism, was replaced by competitive exams. Thus, it was to be hoped, candidates would be appointed on merit rather than patronage. Sadly, however, despite the best intentions, these changes were implemented very slowly and, in fact, the Foreign Office failed to introduce the competitive element into its recruitment process until after the First World War.

That the British army was not the force it once was, was displayed in the early part of the Crimean War and in such humiliating incidents as the Charge of the Light Brigade. Gladstone's Secretary of State for War, Edward Cardwell (1813-86), was tasked with modernising the military. It was evident from Prussia's recent crushing defeat of France that professional soldiers, armed with up-to-date weaponry, were the future and that Britain's traditional employment of gentlemen-soldiers was very much a thing of the past. Therefore, the purchase of officers' commissions was abolished. Previously, the middle and senior ranks in the army were filled by the rich, landowning class and there was no opportunity for the middle class to provide soldiers of high rank. Now, rank would be achieved on merit and military competence rather than on how wealthy the candidate was. Reserve forces with short terms of service for the enlisted men were introduced. Flogging was abolished and Cardwell also brought home 20,000 troops from Britain's self-governing colonies, making it known that these would now have to defend themselves. The War Office now took on more responsibility, and the Commander-in-Chief – at the time the Duke of Cambridge (1819-1904) – was forced to report to it. Cardwell introduced territorialism, dividing the country into 66 districts and recruiting volunteers within those specific areas.

Again, however, not a lot changed. The social make-up of the senior ranks in the army remained decidedly upper class. This was because Cardwell had failed to increase the pay of officers or reduce the cost of being one and people not of the aristocratic or landowning class were hardly likely to be able to afford the position.

Gladstone's Agenda

Queen Victoria persisted in her seclusion following the death of her husband, appearing very rarely in public. Her time was spent between the three royal residences of Balmoral, Osborne House on the Isle of Wight and Windsor Castle. Meanwhile, her son, the Prince of Wales, seemed to be perpetually mired in scandal. The image of the monarchy struggled in the face of these problems, and republican sentiments began to be aired. The writer Walter Bagehot (1826-77) described the royal pair as the 'retired widow' and the 'unemployed youth', stoking the fires of republicanism. This was not helped by the news from France where Napoleon III was overthrown in September 1870 after the defeat by the Prussians and the Third French Republic was proclaimed. Republican clubs opened across Britain and even some leading politicians began to express their doubts about the future of the monarchy in public.

Gladstone was a confirmed royalist and, increasingly concerned about this turn of events, exhorted Her Majesty to emerge from her seclusion and make herself more visible to her subjects. As for the Prince of Wales, he devised a plan to obtain a royal residence in Ireland and install him as a sort of Viceroy there, where he would spend part of each year. It was a double-edged sword; not only would it give the prince something worthwhile to do – although, of course, the position would necessarily be merely honorary – but it might also serve to create closer ties between the people of Ireland and the rest of the United Kingdom. Unfortunately for Gladstone, the queen rejected the idea of an Irish royal residence and the new position for her son. Neither was she willing to appear in public. The royal crisis rumbled on.

There was much else for Gladstone to be getting on with. In 1871, the important Trade Union Act made trade unions legal in the United Kingdom for the first time. The following year, the Ballot Act introduced the secret ballot to elections, reducing the possibility of corrupt practices and outside influence being brought to bear on voters. The powerful temperance lobby was placated with the 1872 Licensing Act that dealt with the licensing of premises for the consumption of alcohol, amongst other things, restricting closing times to midnight in towns and 11 o'clock in rural areas. It created an offence of being drunk in public and also made it an offence to be drunk while in charge of a horse, a cow (or cattle), a steam engine, a carriage or while in possession of a loaded firearm.

Gladstone's government began to run out of steam after about four years in office. There were scandals, too, and financial improprieties that damaged the reputation of the government. Gladstone came in for criticism due to some poor recommendations for high office in the justice system and the Church. The Liberals lost thirty-two seats to the Conservatives in by-elections and, in fact, won only ten in the six years between 1868 and 1874. Eventually, it was Ireland that brought the government down. An Irish University Bill, designed to improve higher education provision in Ireland, was defeated by an alliance of Conservative and Irish MPs. Queen Victoria invited Benjamin Disraeli to form a minority Conservative government.

Wily character that he was, Disraeli rejected the opportunity to form a government, leaving Gladstone to limp on with an increasingly unpopular government that was opposed by a resurgent Conservative Party. He shuffled his cards, placing himself in the role of Chancellor of the Exchequer and installing John Bright as Chancellor of the Duchy of Lancaster. Robert Lowe moved from the Exchequer to the Home Office. One important piece of legislation made it through Parliament around this time, the Supreme Court of Judicature Act 1873 which created two very important British institutions – the Court of Appeal and the High Court of Justice.

Gladstone's decision to call an election early in 1874 surprised many, including his cabinet colleagues. But there was a great deal of disquiet. Nonconformists were unhappy with the Education Act and working-class people were upset by the new trade union laws and especially by the newly introduced restrictions on the consumption of alcohol. Gladstone wanted to abolish income tax in order to attract votes but the cabinet could not agree on this. So, he went to the country. Disraeli berated Gladstone's government for what he called 'incessant and harassing legislation', and insisted that, were he to be elected, he would stop this plethora of law-making, would make every effort to defend the position of the Church of England and would show a little more enthusiasm for foreign policy.

It worked and, for the first time in 33 years, the

Conservative Party was returned to government with a majority and a substantial one, too. The Liberals had a disastrous election, losing 145 seats. The Irish Nationalists of the Home Rule League won seats for the first time, recording victory in 60 seats. This party was led by Irish barrister Isaac Butt (1813-79). Butt was a Protestant, but his party was disgruntled by Gladstone's attitude towards Ireland. The new House of Commons was made up of 350 Conservative MPs, 242 Liberals and 60 Irish Nationalists. Disraeli, therefore, enjoyed a majority of almost 50 seats. Gladstone recognised the irritation expressed by the electorate at the changes in drinks laws. 'We have been swept away,' he said, 'in a torrent of gin and beer.' He resigned as leader of the Liberals, replaced in the Commons by Lord Hartington (1833-1908), son and heir of the 7th Duke of Devonshire and in the Lords by Lord Granville (1815-91).

Disraeli's Government

Half of the first Conservative cabinet since Peel was in office were peers and the remainder were made up of the usual ruling elite. The 15th Earl of Derby, son of the former Prime Minister, the 14th Earl, was given the Foreign Office; Lord Cranborne (1830-1903), later to be Prime Minister under his title Lord Salisbury, was given the role of Secretary of

State for India; and the colonies came under the control of Lord Carnarvon (1831-90). Sir Stafford Northcote (1818-87) was given the Chancellorship and the only non-elite appointee was RA Cross (1823-1914), a banker and solicitor from Lancashire, who was made Home Secretary.

It was a great opportunity for Disraeli. The Liberals were in a state of disarray, the Queen was happier that he was in office rather than Gladstone and, most importantly, this time he had a substantial majority to play with. Not a lot happened immediately, however. Only in 1875 did the wheels of government begin to turn. Cross put forward two bills dealing with the issues raised by the Liberal government's trade union legislation. The Conspiracy and Protection of Property Act decriminalised peaceful picketing while the Employers and Workmen Act did away with the situation where employers had more rights regarding breaches of contract than employees. With these two acts, the trade unions became stronger and workers now had the right to strike action and to collective bargaining. Other acts followed. The Public Health Act 1875 was a significant step forward in public health in Britain, giving local authorities the power to purchase, repair or build sewers, to control water supplies, to regulate cellars and lodging houses and to create by-laws for controlling new streets and buildings. In fact, the difference between houses built before this act and after its passing was dramatic. It required all new residential construction to have running water and an internal drainage system. It also stipulated that every public health authority should have a medical officer and a sanitary inspector. Towns also had to provide paving and lighting. It should be pointed out, however, that these measures were not compulsory; rather, they gave local authorities a model of best practice. Cross also brought in the Sale of Food and Drugs Act which prohibited the use in drugs or food of anything that was dangerous to the health of the consumer. The Artisans' and Labourers' Dwellings Act 1875 came out of the social reform programme that Disraeli had proclaimed during two important speeches at Manchester and Crystal Palace in 1872. It was aimed at what he described as 'the elevation of the people', by which he meant, of course, the working class. This act compelled owners of slum dwellings to sell them to councils which had to pay them compensation; it made loans available from the government at lower than normal interest rates; and it encouraged councils to demolish slum dwellings and allow them to be redeveloped by commercial builders. Although viewed as one of the key pieces of legislation of Disraeli's time in office, this was once again permissive legislation, in that it was not compulsory. Given the cost involved, few councils took any action.

So, although it looked like a year of sweeping social reform, in actuality these acts were less significant than they seemed. Generally speaking, apart from the trade unions legislation, they provided guidelines, guidelines that most local authorities chose to ignore.

Other acts followed in the next few years. A Rivers Pollution Act was one of the first pieces of legislation designed to protect the environment and an Education Act compelled parents to send their children aged between five and ten to school. Sadly, the former was largely ignored and the second was designed to prevent the setting up of school boards in rural areas. By 1876, Disraeli had health problems, suffering from gout, asthma and bronchitis throughout much of that year. When MPs complained that he was no longer fit to lead the government in the Commons, he found a solution by remaining Prime Minister but doing it from the House of Lords where he sat from August 1876 as the Earl of Beaconsfield. When asked later by a friend how he was enjoying being in the Lords, he replied: 'I am dead; dead, but in the Elysian fields.'

Disraeli succeeded where his predecessor had failed in persuading Queen Victoria to return to the public eye. He got on very well with the widowed queen, treating her like a person rather than an institution which had been how Gladstone had related to her. His letters to the queen were unlike any from a Prime Minister to his sovereign before or since and his closeness to her meant that he would always have been able to solve the crisis in the monarchy far more easily than Gladstone. Sympathy for the royal family had increased in the winter of 1871 when Edward had contracted typhoid, the disease that had killed his father. The nation was very concerned, especially when one of the guests at the same house died of the disease. There was a huge upsurge of relief when he recovered and the English composer Arthur Sullivan (1842-1900) composed the *Festival Te Deum*, in thanks for the recovery of the heir to the throne. There was also a service of thanksgiving for the recovery. Disraeli seized this moment to encourage the queen to appear in public again and she agreed to attend the state opening of Parliament in 1876. She appeared at the same event in 1877 and again in 1880.

Disraeli's Foreign Policy

Abroad, and especially with regard to Europe, Disraeli tried to perpetuate the notion that Britain still wielded power and should the need arise, was ready to step in. Meanwhile, he instigated progress in Britain's overseas possessions. While leading the minority Conservative government he inherited from Derby, he had already played a part in creating the Canadian Confederation through the 1867 British North America Act. It brought together the provinces of New Brunswick and Nova Scotia with the colony of Canada, although that was split into the provinces of Quebec and Ontario. A similar process would follow soon after in South Africa and Australia. The purpose was to prevent the United States from casting greedy eyes on the territory to the north, now that the American Civil War was over.

A unified territory would also make it more likely that investors would contribute to the construction of a trans-Canada railway such as had been built in the United States, linking the two coasts. It was also hoped that the provinces of the west of the territory might feel it beneficial to join and they did so in the first two years of the decade. Of course, the United Kingdom also hoped that some of the costs of running the confederation might be passed to it.

Transport was changing the world and the coast-to-coast railways in America and Canada opened up the vast agricultural resources of these nations to Europeans. Transport of another kind also changed the world. The opening of the Suez Canal in Egypt towards the end of 1869, had considerably reduced the journey by sea to India. This was an especial boon for Britain with its connection with the subcontinent. British ships were responsible for 75 per cent of the tonnage passing through the canal.

In 1871, following its great success in the Franco-Prussian War, Germany had become unified as the German Empire under the Chancellorship of Otto von Bismarck's (1815-98) Prussia. As Britain watched impotently from the sidelines, France was supplanted by Germany as the European continent's major power. Like the United States, Germany would come to challenge Britain's standing as the world's leading industrial superpower in the last decades of the nineteenth century.

While Gladstone had largely concentrated on domestic

matters and pursued stability abroad, Disraeli let his colleagues focus on domestic issues while he directed what capability he had, given his declining health, to foreign matters. He was ready to play a role on the world stage and he got his chance in 1875 when Egypt's Khedive, facing bankruptcy, sold his £4 million of shares in the Suez Canal to Britain. Disraeli conducted this business in complete secrecy, helped by the Rothschild Bank, and only once the transaction had been completed did he inform the cabinet and the House of Commons. The route to India, he argued, was far too important to be allowed to fall into the hands of the French government which was already a major shareholder. It was a stunning coup and it would certainly pay off for Britain in the years to come.

In 1858, following the Indian Mutiny of that year, the nominal Mughal Emperor of India had been deposed, and the British government decided to transfer control of British India from the East India Company to the Crown. This would be the beginning of what became known as the British Raj. The East India Company was dissolved on 1 June 1874, and Disraeli decided to offer Queen Victoria the title of 'Empress of India'. She accepted on 1 May 1876. It is suggested that she was particularly keen on the title, perhaps because her daughter, Victoria (1840-1901), had married Crown Prince Frederick who was heir to the German Empire. When he inherited, his wife would become Empress Victoria and would thus outrank her mother who was not at all amused at this prospect. Disraeli introduced the Royal Titles Act 1876 in which the queen was officially recognised as 'Empress of India'. The new title served several purposes. It reinforced Disraeli's claim that Britain was an 'Asiatic power'; it reminded Indians that the rulers of the Indian princely states were fully committed to British hegemony in the region; and it emphasised the fact that Britain was committed to maintaining its rule of the subcontinent, thus sending a warning to Russia that Britain would resolutely defend India and the buffer states that separated the two countries.

Britain persisted in its support for the Ottoman Empire, again as a buffer against Russian aggression and ambition, but in the mid-1870s there were a number of rebellions in the Ottoman-ruled Balkans. These pleased the Habsburg Empire of Austria-Hungary which sought to expand its territory in the region and, of course, Russia looked on supportively from its role as leader of pan-Slavism, a movement that had emerged with the aim of advancing the aspirations of Slavic-speaking peoples. When 12,000 people were reported to have been massacred by Turks in an uprising in Bulgaria in May 1876, Disraeli refused to believe it, describing the reports as 'largely invention'. But a campaign was launched that condemned the actions of the Turks, a campaign supported by Gladstone. He wrote a pamphlet on the matter that sold 200,000 copies in three weeks and gave speeches in support of the persecuted

Christian minorities of the region. Disraeli had completely misjudged the mood of the country and his government never really recovered. Gladstone, on the other hand, was starting to believe that it was time to return to front-line politics. He called Disraeli's politics 'Beaconsfieldism' and wanted to mount a moral crusade against his rival.

In early 1877, Russia declared war on the Ottomans, supported by an Eastern Orthodox coalition consisting of armies from Bulgaria, Serbia, Romania and Montenegro. Russia not only wanted to help the Slavic states, it also sought to regain some of the territory that had been lost in the Crimean War and to re-establish itself in the Black Sea. As Russian victory began to look inevitable, Disraeli ordered the Royal Navy into the Bosphorus and troops were moved to the Mediterranean from India. Lord Carnarvon was against the Ottomans and resigned from the Colonial Office as did the Earl of Derby. Sir Michael Hicks Beach (1837-1916) and Lord Salisbury (formerly Lord Cranborne) filled their roles respectively. Public opinion swung in favour of the Ottomans and it seemed for a while that war between Britain and Russia was once again inevitable. But, before that came to pass, Russia and the Ottoman Empire signed the Treaty of San Stefano in March 1878 that provided for the creation of an autonomous Principality of Bulgaria.

The ensuing peace conference was held in Berlin and represented the largest gathering of European statesmen since the Congress of Vienna in 1815 at the end of the Napoleonic Wars. It was significant in that there were no more major wars between European states for more than a generation. Boundaries of the Slavic states were ratified, the independence of the Ottoman Empire was confirmed and Russian ambition was once again stifled. Britain benefitted by gaining the island of Cyprus from the Ottomans. Disraeli was feted on his return to London with what he called 'peace with honour'. He told the queen that she was now 'the arbiter of Europe'. It sounded good, but was not entirely true.

The Problems of the Late 1870s

In the latter years of the 1870s, Britain suffered a severe industrial and commercial downturn, the end of the prolonged period of growth and stability. Industrial supremacy, the notion of Britain as the 'workshop of the world', now began to look as if it was under threat. There was a significant rise in unemployment and many institutions were ruined, the most spectacular of these being the City of Glasgow Bank, the collapse of which resulted in the demise of dozens of businesses. 1879 was a particularly bad year for business and manufacturing. Agriculture was also enduring a bad time, and four wet summers, coupled with the emergence of the American prairies as a significant player, created a depression amongst British farmers. The price of British wheat plummeted, farmers earned less and were consequently less able to pay their rents. This was, of course, bad news for the Conservatives who relied so much on rural constituencies for support.

The blame for the fall in wheat prices as a result of the import of American crops was, of course, placed by some firmly at the feet of Peel who had removed the protection for British agriculture when he repealed the Corn Laws in 1846. However, although Disraeli agreed with this view, he refused to do what other European countries were doing; namely putting tariffs on imported goods. This was because it would have punished working-class people, especially when around 11 per cent did not have jobs. Naturally, the landed gentry and the elite were dismayed by this. In Ireland, however, it was even worse. There had been some recovery after the Great Famine, but now tenants fell behind in their rents and there was again a huge number of evictions from homes and smallholdings. The Irish Home Rule Party had, until then, not made a great impression on British politics, but that was all changed by a by-election in 1875 that sent Charles Stewart Parnell (1846-91), a 29-year-old Anglo-Irish Protestant landowner and land reform agitator to Westminster. Parnell resolved to make waves in Parliament about Irish landlords and against the Union.

At the same time, Britain suffered some serious reverses in the empire. Gold and diamonds were discovered in South

Africa in the late 1860s. This exacerbated the poor relations between the British in Natal and Cape Colony and the Boers in the Transvaal and the Orange Free State. There were also, of course, the indigenous peoples to be considered. In 1877, to the chagrin of the Boers, Britain annexed the Transvaal. Then Sir Henry Bartle Frere (1815-84), High Commissioner to South Africa, wishing to expand British influence still further, launched a campaign against the powerful Zulu kingdom. Initially, colonial forces were humiliated by the Zulu chief Cetshwayo kaMpande (1826-84) at the Battle of Isandlwana in January 1879, and 1,300 British troops lost their lives. Cetshwayo was eventually defeated in July, captured at the Battle of Ulundi. This brought an end to the Zulu threat.

Such setbacks harmed the standing of the government and further problems in South Asia did even more damage. The Governor-General of India, Lord Lytton (1831-91), took office in 1876 amid concerns about the influence Russia was gaining in Afghanistan. After a Russian delegation was welcomed by the Emir, and a British one was stopped at the border and prevented from meeting the Afghan leader, Lytton issued an ultimatum and then ordered the British army to invade the country, starting the Second Anglo-Afghan War. After a year in which Britain won almost every battle in the war, the Emir gave up control of the passes linking India and Afghanistan to the British. It had been a costly escapade with a great loss of life on both sides, including many civilians. As a result, Britain seized control of Afghan foreign policy in return for guaranteeing to protect Afghanistan from outside interference.

The downturn in the economy and these imperial misadventures played into Gladstone's hands. He gave up his parliamentary seat at Greenwich and said he would fight in the constituency of Midlothian at the next general election, delivering a series of four speeches in which he denounced Disraeli and his government. In orations lasting up to five hours in front of audiences of several thousand people, he lambasted what he called the government's financial incompetence, its failure to deal with domestic issues and its mismanagement of foreign affairs. Widely covered by the press at the time, this campaign has sometimes been described as the first modern political campaign.

Gender and Race in Mid to Late Victorian Britain

There may have been a woman on the throne for much of the nineteenth century, but for women there was little participation in public work or politics. Florence Nightingale was, of course, a notable exception, as was philanthropist, Angela Burdett-Coutts (1814-1906), described by Edward VII as: 'after my mother, the most remarkable woman in the kingdom'. Popularly thought to be the richest heiress in the country – she had inherited a £1.8 million (£150 million in today's terms) fortune from her grandfather – she spent a great deal of her wealth on scholarships, endowments and worthy projects, one of the first of which was a home, created by her and her friend Charles Dickens for young women who had been involved in theft and prostitution. She spent money helping Africans in Africa and people in many other parts of the world. In 1884, she co-founded the London Society for the Prevention of Cruelty to Children which would evolve into the National Society for the Prevention of Cruelty to Children – the NSPCC. Her donations helped to prevent cruelty to animals and children, and she was a pioneer of the idea of social housing.

Of course, these three women – Victoria, Nightingale and Burdett-Coutts – were successful through birth. Victoria was born into royal circles and became queen; Florence Nightingale had the benefit of being born into a prosperous gentry family; and Burdett-Coutts had the advantage of being a wealthy heiress. But, even for such women, it was not easy to succeed in the man's world of the Victorian era. They had their own strategies for dealing with the men by whom they were surrounded. Victoria gained strength from being the daughter of a soldier, even though she was dealing with politicians who were far more worldly-wise and much better educated than her. But she was still of the opinion that women should not have the vote and nor should they be eligible for public office. She suggested that if women were to 'unsex' themselves by claiming equality with men they would become the most hateful, heathen and disgusting of beings and would surely perish without male protection. Florence Nightingale was critical of women's rights activists, believing women were not as capable as men. In fact, she often referred to herself using the masculine form, as 'a man of action' or 'a man of business'.

In reality, during the Victorian period, women remained second-class citizens. Once married – and not marrying was frowned upon until the First World War – a woman became virtually the property of her husband and everything she had before marriage – wealth, possessions – became his to use in whatsoever manner he desired. The only way to avoid this was to establish a trust, an expensive process that could be afforded only by the very well-off. Despite the 1857 Matrimonial Causes Act that abolished the requirement for a private Act of Parliament to obtain a divorce, men had an easier job divorcing their spouses than women did. One act of adultery by his wife could give a man a divorce but the law did not even acknowledge that adultery by men was an offence. Society turned a blind eye to men enjoying sexual relations with as many women as they wanted; were a woman to behave in the same manner, she was ostracised.

Basically, the genders operated in different areas. It was very much Queen Victoria's idea that the woman was responsible for the domestic part of a marriage while the man should be involved in public work such as politics or government, business or other work. The woman had to bear children and then look after them and the household. Naturally, this suffocated many women who felt restricted by their domestic responsibilities. Other women thrived by being what the poet Coventry Patmore (1823-96) described in one poem as 'The Angel in the House'. 'Man must be pleased; but him to please/Is woman's pleasure...' Nonetheless, in the middle of the Victorian era, a third of the workforce still consisted of women, mostly unmarried. Employment as domestic servants or as workers in the textile industry was particularly common.

Change for women was afoot, however. In 1874, the Women's Protective and Provident League was founded, encouraging women to form trade unions, and such organisations were recognised by the Trades Union Congress. Even so, unionised women remained a tiny percentage of the female workforce. In 1870, the Married Women's Property Act enabled women to keep their own wages if they worked. After 1882, they were permitted to keep their property separate from that of their husbands after marriage. In terms of enfranchisement, a small step was taken in 1869, when the Municipal Franchise Act gave the vote in local elections to women paying rates. Women had for some time been eligible for election to school boards, but from 1875, they were permitted to take on the role of Poor Law Guardian.

One acknowledged authority on the improvement in education standards for girls and women was Frances Buss (1827-94), from 1850 to 1890 head of the North London Collegiate School which offered secondary education to girls, many of whom were from the lower middle classes. Buss spent her life fighting for women to take every opportunity they could. She argued for girls to be competitively examined, just like boys, and encouraged women to take roles on school boards and in local government. In fact, around this time, a number of schools for girls opened their doors, including Cheltenham Ladies' College which was established in 1853 with 82 pupils. The Schools Enquiry Commission of 1864 reported a 'general deficiency' in the provision of secondary education for girls. In response, Maria Grey (1816-1906) and her sister Emily Shirreff (1814-97) launched the National Union for Improving the Education of Women of All Classes, later known as the Women's Education Union. The Union sought to establish cheap day schools for all girls, regardless of class, above the level of elementary education, and was behind the Girls' Public Day School Company, founded in 1872. The first school it opened was in Chelsea in 1873 and, by 1905, it operated 37 schools for girls across the country. Higher education also saw increasing opportunities for women. At Cambridge, Girton College was founded in 1869 and Newnham in 1871, and at Oxford, Lady Margaret Hall opened in 1878 while Somerville College welcomed women students from 1879.

Women were, of course, a long way from obtaining the right to vote in parliamentary elections. The first organisation to enter the fray in that area was the Manchester Women's Suffrage Committee and other such organisations followed in the nation's cities. Millicent Fawcett (1847-1929) was one of the more prominent members of the London branch of the Women's Suffrage Committee and her sister was Elizabeth Garrett Anderson, a doctor who had qualified in Paris and would be the first woman member of the British Medical Association in 1873. Like many women, the sisters had been impressed by the work of John Stuart Mill who, while a Member of Parliament, had delivered an impassioned, but ultimately unsuccessful plea for women's suffrage in the Commons at the time of the Second Reform Act. He expounded his thinking in his 1869 publication, *The Subjugation of Women*, in which he insisted that by excluding women from the franchise and limiting their opportunities, society itself was suffering. 'Under whatever conditions,' he wrote, 'and within whatever limits, men are admitted to the suffrage, there is not a shadow of justification for not admitting women under the same.'

Unfortunately, as attitudes towards women began to soften, they undoubtedly became less tolerant where race was concerned. Scientists had something to say about race and the gradations of mankind. The pseudo-science of phrenology claimed that the position of the various races on the human evolutionary scale was shown by the structure of the skull and facial angles and jaw formation. It led to a debate as to whether there had been one creation for all of mankind – monogenism – or a number of creations – polygenism. The latter contributed to distasteful theories and led to racial stereotyping.

Racial prejudice was not just about colour, however. The Irish, for instance, were often portrayed as brutish and considered inferior. Depictions in *Punch* show them with ape-like or even demonic features, and a long jaw, a signifier to phrenologists of a race lower in the evolutionary order. John Beddoe (1826-1911), later President of the Anthropological Institute, an organisation that promoted a doctrine of scientific racism, wrote that men of genius had less prominent jawbones, while those of the Irish and Welsh were long – 'prognathous', as he termed it. The Celt, he claimed, was, in fact, a close relation of Cromagnon man who, according to Beddoe's outrageous argument, was associated with the 'Africanoid'. Such views were disdained by most serious scientists but were widely disseminated. The writer Charles Kingsley wrote shockingly in an 1868 letter to his wife: 'I am haunted by the human chimpanzees I saw [in Ireland]… to see white chimpanzees is awful; if they were black one would not feel it so much.' He stopped believing in the intrinsic equality and unity of mankind, declaring 'that the differences of race are so great, that certain races, e.g. the Irish Celts, seem quite unfit for self-government'.

Of course, racism was prevalent in the wider British Empire, the supposed inferiority of other races being used as a tool to justify imperial ambition. The British believed themselves to be the apogee of civilisation and also that it was possible to help other races approach such a level of civilisation. To begin with, it was thought that this could be achieved through missionaries preaching the word of God and converting native peoples to Christianity or by supplying them with the wherewithal to live. This could also mean abolishing local customs and renouncing 'native' beliefs. As the century wore on, however, the belief grew that there did, in fact, exist a racial hierarchy. The problem with this view was that there was no opportunity for one race to climb the hierarchy. It was a view that twisted somewhat Darwin's notion of 'survival of the fittest'. Darwin at no point said that one race was superior to another, but some suggested that the people of Britain enjoyed the advantages they did because they were, quite simply, from a superior race that had proved itself 'the fittest'. Many, including Benjamin Disraeli, insisted that race was the key to how society worked. 'All was race', Disraeli claimed. One might well imagine that for Disraeli, a Jew, after all, who had reached the pinnacle of British society, race would be very important. In fact, he manufactured a false lineage for himself, claiming he was of Spanish and Venetian Jewish heritage. This conveniently ignored his mainly Italian ancestry.

Dr James Hunt (1833-69), President of the Anthropological Society of Great Britain, was of the opinion that there were 'about six races below the negro, and six above him'. The explorers who were the first Europeans to visit parts of Africa often regarded Africans as little different to animals. Sir Richard Burton (1821-90), who, with John Hanning Speke (1827-64), had been the first Europeans to visit the African Great Lakes in the Rift Valley, believed that Africans suffered from arrested mental development and belonged to 'the lower breeds of mankind'. He considered them to be 'a futile race of barbarians, drunken and immoral'.

Across the empire, attitudes towards subjected peoples were hardening. The 1857 rebellion in India against the British East India Company had a great impact on people, shaking confidence in the wisdom of empire and especially in the subcontinent. There was a growing suspicion of the South Asian and a view that as a race South Asians were deceitful and cruel. 'A general feeling of repugnance' was how Indian Viceroy, Lord Canning (1812-62) described the Englishman's attitude to Indians, immediately after the Indian Mutiny. There were also problems with the Maoris in New Zealand which tainted the view of the indigenous people there.

The idea that the British were bringing civilisation to backward peoples was exemplified by an incident in Jamaica. In October 1865, there was a small-scale uprising, known as the Morant Bay Rebellion that resulted in the deaths of 439 of the inhabitants of the island. 600 were flogged and 354 court-martialled; 1,000 houses were burned down. Edward John Eyre (1815-1901), Governor of Jamaica, supervised the quashing of the rebellion and had the island turned into a Crown Colony with an appointed legislature. The legislature sanctioned martial law and, importantly for Eyre, passed an Act of Indemnity which stipulated that all the actions to suppress the uprising had been carried out in 'good faith'. These events stirred up a huge controversy in Britain, where some people insisted that Eyre be arrested for the murder of George William Gordon, a mixed-race colonial assemblyman, who had been involved in the rebellion and executed for the part he played in it. Amongst those advocating Eyre's arrest were Charles Darwin, John Bright, Thomas Henry Huxley and the philosopher and political theorist Herbert Spencer (1820-1903). Eyre was condemned by many as a racist, while others heaped praise upon him for his defence of Christian civilisation. The debate on the matter became enmeshed in the parliamentary debates of the second Reform Bill. Those who supported Eyre's stance warned that the extension of the franchise would result in the kind of uprisings and atrocities that had occurred in Jamaica. Those who opposed his actions wished to extend the franchise because they feared that violence would be the result of failing to do so. Although a royal commission criticised Eyre for his actions, the *Times* described the Morant Bay Rebellion as worse than the Indian Mutiny because it proved that 'the Negro' was not fit to govern himself.

Thus, from this time onwards, racial attitudes toughened and it was no longer widely believed that the various non-white races that Britain had conquered could be improved and attain the standards of civilisation that prevailed in Britain and Europe. Self-government for these regions was now completely out of the question. Indigenous people, it was suggested, could only be employed in subordinate roles and those who were educated could no longer be trusted. This served to place an obvious wedge between the colonial ruling class and the people they governed.

Literature in the 1870s

Literature took up the issues of gender and race in books such as George Eliot's *Middlemarch* (1872) in which she examines the unfulfilled life of Dorothea Brooke, condemned to a loveless marriage to a controlling man who excludes her from his intellectual pursuits. As he had done in his 1859 novel, *The Woman in White*, Wilkie Collins was critical of the attitude towards women in *Man and Wife*, published in 1870.

Collins also wrote *The Moonstone* (1869), considered by many to be the first example of the detective novel. The stone of the title is based on the spectacular Koh-I-Noor diamond which was ceded to Queen Victoria following the annexation of the Kingdom of Punjab by the East India Company. The book also dealt with the iniquities of British rule in the subcontinent. Charles Dickens's novel, *The Mystery of Edwin Drood*, was to be published in 12 instalments from April 1870 to February 1871, but Dickens was the victim of a stroke in June 1870 from which he never recovered. The story, therefore, remained unfinished. Thus ended the career of the writer regarded by many as the greatest English novelist. He created some of the greatest and most memorable characters in all fiction and achieved unprecedented popularity during his lifetime.

In 1871, another of the era's great writers, Lewis Carroll – the pen name of the scholar and teacher, Charles Dodgson (1832-98) – published *Through the Looking Glass, and What Alice Found There*, his sequel to his 1865 book, *Alice's Adventures in Wonderland*. *The Hunting of the Snark* followed in 1876. These fantastic tales are amongst the finest examples of the literary nonsense genre which was also represented by Edward Lear (1812-88) in his *Nonsense Songs, Stories, Botany, and Alphabets*, also published in 1871. It included his most famous nonsense song, *The Owl and the Pussycat*.

Samuel Butler (1835-1902) initially published the Utopian satire, *Erewhon* (1872), anonymously. The title – 'nowhere' spelt backwards with the letters 'w' and 'h' transposed –

is the name of a country that the novel's protagonist has supposedly discovered. Butler satirises certain elements of Victorian society, such as the punishment of criminals, religion and the idea that human beings are the most important thing in the universe. When Butler revealed himself as the author, he became a well-known figure.

The novelist Thomas Hardy (1840-1928) was highly critical of the society in which he lived, and especially the treatment of rural people like those who lived in his native Dorset. Although he considered himself primarily a poet, he gained fame as a novelist with books such as *Far from the Madding Crowd*, published in 1876. Often set in the fictional county of Wessex, Hardy's novels feature characters that are generally tragic figures who undergo difficulties as a result of their private passions and the social circumstances in which they live. *Far from the Madding Crowd* was his first major critical and popular success, describing the life and relationships of farmer Bathsheba Everdene. Hardy's sixth novel, *The Return of the Native*, followed in 1878, in twelve monthly instalments in the magazine *Belgravia*. It deals with the tragedy of romantic illusion and the way that people often fail to take responsibility for their own destinies.

Black Beauty, the only novel by Anna Sewell (1820-78) was published in 1877, and became one of the most popular children's books in English literature. Written when she was dying, Sewell intended it for people who work with horses and said that its 'special aim was to induce kindness, sympathy, and an understanding treatment of horses'. It had an effect. For instance, the book featured the use of bearing reins which are very painful for horses. These fell out of favour in the years after the book's publication.

In 1870, the Reverend E Cobham Brewer (1810-97) published *Brewer's Dictionary of Phrase and Fable*, for those who had not benefited from higher education, but who were still curious about the origins of phrases and historical or literary references. Also in the world of reference books, 1872 saw the publication of the *Chambers Dictionary* by Edinburgh siblings, William and Robert Chambers. It would later go on to become the dictionary of choice for crossword setters and solvers, and for players of Scrabble.

6

The 1880s:
Carving up the World

The Return of Gladstone

Throughout 1879, Disraeli's health continued to fail. He was 45 minutes late for his speech at the Lord Mayor's Dinner at the Guildhall in November of that year due to ill health. When he told his audience that he intended to speak at the event the following year, after the general election that was due, they sniggered. Disraeli's frailty and Gladstone's astonishing campaign made them think this unlikely.

In the event, they were right. The Conservatives lost 113 seats and, much to the chagrin of Queen Victoria, Gladstone's Liberals were returned to power. Instead, she hoped that Lord Hartington, leader of the Liberals in the House of Commons, or Lord Granville, leader in the Lords, might become Prime Minister. Gladstone had already intimated to them, however, that he wished to do the job once again, and, it seemed that the country wanted him back as well. Victoria, therefore, had no choice and at 70 years of age, Gladstone formed his second government, assuming the roles of Chancellor of the Exchequer and Leader of the House of Commons himself. Lord Granville took the Foreign Office and Lord Kimberley (1826-1902) the job of Colonial Secretary. Hartington was Secretary of State for India. The make-up of the cabinet was as ever decidedly aristocratic, with four other peers, including the Duke of Argyll as Lord Privy Seal. One important cabinet debutant was Joseph Chamberlain (1836-1914) as President of the Board of Trade. He had been Mayor of Birmingham and was the founder of the National Liberal Federation which was trying to unify the Liberal Party under one umbrella. Unfortunately for Gladstone, his cabinet would end up at war with itself within a few years.

For the moment, however, all looked rosy for the Liberals, especially as the Tories seemed once again to be in disarray. Disraeli's health finally gave way in April 1881 and he died, replaced as leader by two men, as the Liberals had earlier done. In the Commons, they were led by Sir Stafford Northcote, while in the Lords the Marquess of Salisbury took the role. It was not a successful team, however. Northcote had once been Gladstone's private secretary and he failed completely to present a challenge to his erstwhile mentor. Salisbury was totally out-of-touch with the new electorate created by the Second Reform Act. In an essay published in the *Quarterly Review*, he described those who had joined the electorate recently, as, amongst other things, ignorant and unpatriotic.

There was a fear in the country, as expressed passionately by Salisbury, that the Union was at that moment in danger, that the widening of the franchise put everything in jeopardy – the traditional hierarchy and the homes and possessions of all – that class war was inevitable. Many Conservative MPs and peers shared his gloomy outlook for the country and even Queen Victoria worried what Gladstone might make of her position. The claims were exaggerated, however, and, in reality, Gladstone wanted to preserve the status quo just as much as Salisbury.

A Better Life

Despite the downturn in the economy that lasted from about 1873 to 1896, some things were improving for the nation. Between 1871 and 1881, the population increased from 32 million to 38 million. But many were moving from the countryside to towns and more than two-thirds of Britons now lived in urban environments. Parts of the economy were growing, especially in the heavy industry sector. The number of people involved in the coal industry had increased from 216,000 in 1861 to 495,000 by the start of the 1880s. Innovations in iron, steel and engineering had also rapidly developed these industries, contributing to the further expansion of the railways and shipbuilding. Exports flourished, almost half of them being textiles while almost another 25 per cent were made up of coal, iron and steel or engineering products. The figures for Britain's global manufacturing performance were astonishing. Its share was 23 per cent in 1881 and the country was also responsible for 44 per cent of the total exported goods in the world.

People were still emigrating, however, to the United States, Canada, Australia, New Zealand and South Africa. In the 1880s, 3.5 million left these shores. Meanwhile, money was also leaving the country, to be invested in ventures both inside and outside the empire. British overseas assets outstripped every other nation in the world, increasing from £1,000 million in 1880 to about £2,000 million by the end of the century. The financial sector, too, was growing. The City of London was the most important and most powerful financial centre in the world, employing more and more people in banking, insurance, shipping, and in the commodity markets as well as the London Stock Exchange.

Buoyant industry inevitably brought prosperity to the country's inhabitants and people were undoubtedly enjoying a better standard of living than previously.

At the same time, many of the great families were also benefitting from this prosperity, drawing substantial incomes from property in urban areas and from mining royalties. The professions that employed the middle classes were increasing in number. Indeed, those employed in public service and the professions rose from 600,000 in 1871 to 800,000 at the end of the 1880s. This would contribute to the fact that future politicians would often be lawyers, men such as David Lloyd George (1863-1945) and HH Asquith (1852-1928). Office positions for lower middle-class workers also grew in number. The working class, too, benefitted. In the last quarter of the nineteenth century, wages went up by a third which meant that they lived well and ate better than ever, a great benefit for their health and well-being. The death rate began to decline, and epidemics of diseases such as cholera and typhus became things of the past. Violent crime declined, too, partly because of the uniformed police force that people now welcomed rather than saw as something to be feared.

Examples of Victorian paternalism can be seen in the pioneering work of men such as William Lever (1851-1925) and George Cadbury (1839-1922). Lever established Lever Brothers with his brother James (1854-1916) in 1886, manufacturing Sunlight Soap and many other well-known brands. In 1887, he bought 56 acres of land on the Wirral in Cheshire where he built his factory and a model village for his workforce. Port Sunlight village provided housing of a good standard, supporting his belief that this would render his workers happier and, therefore, more productive. Nonetheless, living at Port Sunlight meant adherence to strict and sometimes intrusive rules and, of course, when a worker lost his or her job, the home was also lost. George Cadbury was a Quaker who, with his brother, Richard (1835-1899), took over the family business making cocoa and chocolate in 1861. In 1893, like Lever, they built a model village for their workers, named Bournville, south of Birmingham.

The products these two companies were producing were just two of the many created around this time, a lot of which are still being sold today. Retail chains also began to appear, such as Lipton's, Home and Colonial Stores, and Boots the chemist. Cooperative Wholesale Societies served the working class, selling goods at low prices and espousing a powerful moral imperative. The Rochdale Society of Equitable Pioneers, founded in 1844, is universally recognised as the first such enterprise but by 1881, there were half a million members and a turnover of £15 million. Ten years later these numbers had grown inexorably to more than 1.5 million members and turnover had risen to £50 million.

But, if life had improved greatly by the 1880s, there was still a great deal of social unrest, caused by factors such as unemployment and squalid living conditions. In the middle years of the decade, workers protested angrily in the streets of Britain. Riots broke out in February 1886 in Central London; shops were looted and a huge amount of damage was done. In November 1887, a vast demonstration took place in Trafalgar Square on a day that became known as 'Bloody Sunday'. The protest, organised by the Social Democratic Federation and the Irish National League, was about unemployment and the situation in Ireland. There were violent clashes between police and demonstrators armed with iron bars and knives. Four hundred were arrested and seventy-five people were seriously injured. The following year, one of the most famous serial killers in criminal history was on the loose. 'Jack the Ripper' brutally murdered five prostitutes between August and November 1888 in the Whitechapel area of London. In 1889, London's dockers came out on strike, an action that was widely supported across the country and across the empire. The strike was over a demand for what was termed the 'dockers' tanner', a rate of sixpence an hour as well as bonuses that were paid for working quickly. The strike was peaceful, with large marches which won sympathy for the strikers. The general manager at Millwall Docks gave evidence on the physical condition of the dockers to a parliamentary committee:

'The poor fellows are miserably clad, scarcely with a boot on their foot, in a most miserable state... These are men who come to work in our docks who come on without having a bit of food in their stomachs, perhaps since the previous day; they have worked for an hour and have earned 5d.; their hunger will not allow them to continue: they take the 5d. in order that they may get food, perhaps the first food they have had for twenty-four hours.'

The 100,000 strikers won the day and their action, acknowledged as a milestone in the development of the British labour movement, led to the establishment of strong trade unions amongst dockers and the growth of unions for casual, unskilled workers. The 1888 strike by women and girls at match manufacturer, Bryant and May, demonstrated this new mood, as did the organisation of London gas workers at the same time. It was the start of what were called 'New Unions', as trade union protection was broadened to include the unskilled. The Trades Union Congress now welcomed 1.5 million workers, compared to around 650,000 two years previously and the number of trade unions more than doubled.

Other organisations had been formed by socialist intellectuals during the 1880s to try to improve conditions for workers and create social justice. Textile designer, writer and social activist, William Morris (1834-96), was one of the founders of the revolutionary organisation, the Socialist League, in 1884. This was a breakaway offshoot from the Social Democratic Federation, founded in 1881 under the influence of Karl Marx's *Communist Manifesto* by writer and politician, Henry Hyndman (1842-1921). The Fabian Society, an organisation that wanted to advance socialist ideas democratically, was founded by, amongst others, the writer HG Wells (1866-1946), the playwright George Bernard Shaw (1856-1950), and the social reformers Beatrice (1858-1943) and Sidney Webb (1859-1947).

The National Agricultural Labourers' Union was created in 1872 by Joseph Arch (1826-1919). He observed first-hand the conditions in which farm labourers and their families had to live, as described by the Countess of Warwick in Arch's autobiography:

'Bread was dear, and wages down to starvation point; the labourers were uneducated, under-fed, underpaid; their cottages were often unfit for human habitation, the sleeping and sanitary arrangements were appalling... In many a country village the condition of the labourer and his family was but little removed from that of the cattle they tended.'

Arch's aim was to improve the wages and conditions of farm workers and, within two years of its establishment, it had 80,000 members. There were some improvements in the lives of farm labourers, but economic depression made it difficult for the union to have any real bargaining power and numbers dwindled. However, his union helped more than 40,000 members to emigrate with their families to Australia and Canada. He also campaigned for electoral reform, resulting in the 1884 Representation of the People Act which further extended the franchise to all men – not just those living in boroughs – paying an annual rent of £10 or more, or owning land valued at £10 or more. It grew the British electorate to 5,500,000. Arch took advantage of it in 1885, by winning the North-West Norfolk seat for the Liberal Party, the first agricultural labourer to enter the House of Commons. He lost it in 1886, but won it again in 1892, one of 12 working-class men to become MPs that year. He eventually retired from Parliament in 1900.

Meanwhile, in Ireland there was what was called a 'Land War'. Tenants refused to pay their rents and landlords answered that with many evictions which led to violence. This brought renewed calls for Home Rule for Ireland and the agitation against landlords also spread to Wales. The equivalent in Scotland was the 'Crofters' War' which started in 1882 and was coloured by the bitter history of the Highland Clearances. In the Highlands, deer forests had taken the land previously given over to sheep, meaning there was a shortage of land for grazing and arable planting. Crofters voted for the first time in 1885, and with the support of their lowland sympathisers, succeeded in getting a Crofters Act through Parliament the following year. It gave them security of tenure and established a commission to fix fair rents. Unfortunately, though, it did nothing to open up more land for the crofters. This particular agitation, supported by Lowlanders as well as Highlanders, represented an important step in the establishment of a modern Scottish consciousness.

Forster's Education Act appeared to have made a difference and many working-class people could now read a wide variety of newspapers and magazines. Other entertainment was provided by the music hall which had its origins in the eighteenth century. It developed in the new-style saloon bars of pubs that emerged in the 1830s. In the 1850s, music halls were built in the grounds of public houses and, unlike at the theatre, patrons could sit at tables and drink alcohol while performances took place. The first true music hall, the Canterbury, opened in Westminster Bridge Road in May 1852 and many more followed. By the end of the 1880s, 45,000 people attended London's 35 music halls each night.

In 1887, Queen Victoria celebrated 50 years on the throne, a Golden Jubilee marked by lavish celebrations. On 20 June, a royal banquet was held, attended by 50 foreign kings and princes, along with the governing heads of Britain's overseas colonies and dominions. The queen recorded the event in her diary:

'Had a large family dinner. All the Royalties assembled in the Bow Room, and we dined in the Supper-room, which looked splendid with my buffet covered with the gold plate. The table was a large horse-shoe one, with many lights on it. The King of Denmark took me in, and Willy of Greece sat on my other side. The Princes were all in uniform, and the Princesses were all beautifully dressed. Afterwards we went into the Ballroom, where my band played.'

The next day, she paraded from Buckingham Palace to Westminster Abbey for a service of thanksgiving and, returning to the palace, she appeared on the balcony where she was cheered by the large crowd that had gathered. Another banquet followed that night, at which she wore a gown embroidered with thistles, roses and shamrocks. After she had greeted a procession of diplomats and Indian princes, there was a large fireworks display in the gardens of the palace. The celebration gave people cause to consider the 50 years of Victoria's rule and realise the great changes that had occurred in the United Kingdom and the British Empire in that time.

Two Indian Muslims were employed by the queen as waiters at the banquet. One of them, Abdul Karim (1863-1909), became her clerk and she affectionately nicknamed him 'Munshi' (meaning 'clerk' or 'teacher'). He taught her Urdu but there was horror at the palace amongst Victoria's family and her staff, some even suggesting that he was a spy for the Muslim Patriotic League. Others were concerned that he was making Her Majesty favour Muslims over Hindus. Victoria put the complaints about the Munshi down to nothing more than racial prejudice and he remained her servant until her death when he returned to India with a pension.

The Scramble for Africa

There was a growing feeling as the 1880s progressed, that, in order to protect Britain's precious asset, India, it would be necessary to expand imperial holdings in Africa. At the beginning of the decade, Britain's presence was felt only in some bases established to stop slavery and, of course, in southern Africa where, in 1881, the Boers defeated a British force at Majuba Hill, not long after the setback of the disaster of Isandlwana. There was outrage in Parliament and across the country and the ensuing peace talks were acrimonious, leading to an unsatisfactory outcome in the shape of the Pretoria Convention which was signed in August 1881. Under this agreement, the South African Republic regained its self-government, but it would only be under British 'suzerainty'. For the British this meant control of foreign policy and some influence over the way that the Boers treated the black peoples of South Africa. The Boers understood it in another way. Three years later, there were renegotiations that resulted in the 1884 London

Convention in which suzerainty was relinquished by Britain and a number of other concessions were made. The Boers remained discontented, however, irritated by Britain's influence in the region and resentful of the way in which the British failed to show respect for their customs and beliefs. They began to ignore the frontiers that had been established and settled in the lands of the indigenous African peoples. The situation was becoming ever more incendiary and would inevitably lead to conflict in the future.

Meanwhile, since Disraeli's purchase of an interest in the Suez Canal in 1879, the waterway had been controlled by France and Britain in a system known as 'Dual Control'. Ordinary Egyptians were horrified by this state of affairs and felt humiliated by foreign interests running one of their prize assets. This led to a revolt in February 1882 against the Egyptian leader, Khedive Tewfik (1852-92), led by Colonel Ahmed 'Urabi (1841-1911). Alarmed, British officials in Egypt became concerned that Egypt's economy was on the brink of collapse and that 'Urabi, Prime Minister of Egypt from July to September 1882, would default on his country's massive debt and try to gain control of the canal. In terms of imports and exports, Egypt was also very important to Britain. Ships of the British and French navies arrived off the coast of Egypt in May, causing Egyptians to riot and kill six British-born people. The French vessels withdrew, but the British remained and bombarded Alexandria. British troops were sent and, led by General Garnet Wolseley

(1833-1913), defeated an Egyptian force at Tel-el-Kebir in September. The captured 'Urabi was sent into exile and the British assumed control of Egypt under Sir Evelyn Baring (1841-1917) as British Consul General. Although the British consistently insisted that they were leaving Egypt, they failed to do so and, when the First World War began in 1914, the country was declared a protectorate. It was just the first such military intervention in Africa, of which many would follow, especially by the Germans and the French who were, perhaps understandably, angered by what they saw as the duplicity of the British in Egypt. To the delight of Germany and Bismarck, the relationship between France and Britain would remain damaged for the next 15 years.

In the Sudan, nominally under the control of the Egyptian Khedive, there was mounting resentment at British intervention in Egypt and especially the increasing influence of Western habits and customs. The main protagonist in this unrest was a quasi-religious figure, Muhammad Ahmad bin Abd Allah, popularly known as the Mahdi (1844-85). His army defeated the Egyptians in 1883, at which point British subjects were evacuated from the Sudan. General Charles Gordon (1833-85) had fought in the Crimean War and had subsequently made his name in China, as leader of the 'Ever Victorious Army', a Chinese force led by Europeans. He had been employed by the Khedive in 1873, with the approval of the British government, and had been Governor-General of the

Sudan where he was kept busy fighting the slave trade and suppressing revolts. He returned to Britain in 1880 but four years later was sent to Khartoum, capital of the Sudan, to try to enable soldiers who had remained loyal and civilians to escape. After ensuring the escape of around 2,500 people, Gordon defied his orders, and remained in Khartoum with a small force. He was besieged there for almost a year, thrilling the British public with his escapades. The government, dismayed by his actions, was persuaded by public opinion to send a relief force, in July 1885, under General Wolseley, but it was too late. Khartoum had fallen and Gordon had been killed two days before the relief expedition's arrival. He became an instant martyr for the empire and Gladstone was lambasted for this disaster and the others that had recently befallen his government. But the 'Scramble for Africa', as it was called, was now well underway. King Leopold of the Belgians had for some time had his eyes set on the Congo; the French occupied Tunisia in 1881 and a few years earlier had begun to interfere in Senegal in West Africa; and Germany, had adopted a policy of *Weltpolitik* (World Politics) to make the country into a global power. One element of this was to acquire overseas colonies and Germany was looking at territories in Southwest Africa, East Africa and the Cameroons.

The Congress of Berlin, held between November 1884 and February 1885, settled many of the issues surrounding African colonisation. The continent was quite simply carved up amongst the powers. British claims to Somaliland, Bechuanaland and Nigeria were all ratified while France, Germany and Belgium also got what they wanted. Trading interests were protected and, in the case of Bechuanaland, the northern route to the Cape was protected. The irony was that these were gained for the empire by a Liberal government that had expressed no desire to add to British imperial possessions.

There was similar land-grabbing in the Far East. The French took control of Indochina while the Dutch seized control of Sumatra. The British wanted control of Borneo which was of strategic importance, flanking, as it did, the major sea routes from Singapore to China. They chartered the British North Borneo Company to govern the area but with the Sultans of Sulu and Brunei nominally ruling. There were more annexations in South Asia in 1885. Upper Burma was taken, after the king, who had been making overtures to the French, was declared a tyrant, and a British force of 10,000 was victorious in the Third Anglo-Burmese War.

In 1887, a conference of colonial prime ministers took place around the time of Queen Victoria's Golden Jubilee. More than a hundred delegates participated and although the meeting was purely deliberative, there were some decisions. Australia and New Zealand agreed to pay £126,000 annually towards the costs of the Royal Navy and it was agreed that a telegraph cable be laid between Australia and Canada.

As the British government tried to continue to build its empire on the cheap, charters were issued to several companies in Africa – the Royal Niger Company, to establish British claims to the territory around the Lower Niger River, and the Imperial British East Africa Company, to oversee the region that would become Kenya and Uganda. Cecil Rhodes (1853-1902), who had made his fortune from diamonds and gold, was granted a charter for the British South Africa Company so that he could exploit what he believed to be gold deposits in Mashonaland before the Portuguese got there from their neighbouring colonies, Angola and Mozambique. The mineral riches he anticipated failed to materialise in any of these territories and the relationship of company employees to local people was terrible and often violent. The British government was left with little option other than to intervene and take control of the lands for which these companies were responsible. In other places, Britain, France and Germany came to arrangements and sometimes swapped territories to make things work more efficiently. Britain, for instance, handed Germany the island of Heligoland in the North Sea in exchange for the island of Zanzibar.

Much of the annexation carried out around this time was pre-emptive, done merely to prevent France, Germany or Portugal getting their hands on the territory. Of course, there might be no value in it at all, but the question was how bad would it look if a region slipped through British fingers and turned out to possess valuable minerals, like South Africa? The acquisitions therefore continued.

The Irish Question

Gladstone's aim 'to pacify Ireland', when he took office in 1868, was no closer to success by 1882. The Land War had brought renewed violence, but there was a new man at the helm of the movement to gain Home Rule for Ireland. Charles Stewart Parnell, leader of the Home Rule Party, threw his support behind the tenants fighting the Land War. It was from this time that the word 'boycott' first came into use. It was taken from the name of the hapless land agent for Lord Erne (1802-85), Captain Charles Boycott (1832-97). Boycott was ostracised by the local community in the Lough Mask area of County Mayo. Lord Erne's tenants were the first to stop their rent payments, launching the campaign for the three Fs – fair rent, fixity of tenure and free sale. Boycott was refused service in shops and all other services were withdrawn from him. He wrote to the *Times* and the case became a *cause célèbre* in the British press. Eventually, 50 Orangemen from County Cavan arrived to harvest the crops on Lord Erne's land, in defiance of the Catholic tenants, and more than 1,000 troops of the Royal Hussars were deployed to keep the peace. It is estimated that it cost around £10,000 to harvest a crop worth just £500.

Parnell took the struggle to the very heart of the government, Westminster, with a programme of obstruction and disruption, making it increasingly difficult for the government to do its business. When, in 1881, Gladstone tried to introduce legislation for Ireland that would suspend *habeas corpus* and give greater powers to the Chief Secretary for Ireland, the government minister responsible for governing Ireland, Parnell's MPs kept Parliament sitting for 41 hours, delaying the progress of the bill. Eventually, the Speaker had to bring proceedings to a close with the legislation still not on the statute books, although it was eventually passed. Parnell was jailed with some colleagues in October 1881 for 'sabotaging the Land Act' after publishing a *No Rent Manifesto*. In prison, however, he came to the conclusion that Home Rule for Ireland would never be achieved through militancy. He promised the government to stop the violence and to cooperate with it, providing the government settled the issue of 'rent arrears' by allowing 100,000 Irish tenants to appeal for fair rents at the land courts, an agreement that became known as the Kilmainham Treaty. He was released in May 1882 and returned to constitutional politics, reorganising his party as the Irish National League with a programme that combined modern agrarianism and Home Rule. He worked closely with the Catholic Church, realising that its endorsement for Home Rule was vital. Although uneasy with the INL, the Church acknowledged Parnell's party had Church interests at heart and, by 1885, the organisation boasted 1,200 branches throughout Ireland. At the same time, Parnell focused on the Home Rule League, the parliamentary group within Westminster which he would lead for the next decade. Again, he restructured it, along the lines of the INL. Previously, the party's MPs had voted against it on occasion. Some did not even attend Westminster, citing the cost of travel and subsistence once there. MPs, after all, were not paid until 1911. He changed the name to the Irish Parliamentary Party and ensured that candidates were selected who would take their seats in Westminster.

Many saw the Kilmainham Treaty as a capitulation by Gladstone. Lord Cowper (1834-1905), Lord Lieutenant of Ireland and William Edward Forster, Chief Secretary for Ireland, resigned, to be replaced respectively by Earl Spencer (1835-1910) and Lord Frederick Cavendish (1836-82). Cavendish, however, was murdered while walking in Phoenix Park, just hours after arriving in Dublin, by a group of Irish terrorists belonging to the Irish Republican organisation, the Irish National Invincibles. The Permanent Under-Secretary in the Irish Office, Thomas H Burke (1829-82) was also killed in the attack. Naturally, there was outrage and Gladstone was placed in a very difficult position, his contact with Parnell condemned everywhere. Parnell, for his part, was horrified and offered to resign his seat at Westminster.

A Liberal Victory

On 8 June 1885, the government was defeated on an amendment to the budget by Sir Michael Hicks Beach. Gladstone took this defeat as a vote of no confidence and resigned on the following day. A fortnight later, Lord Salisbury formed a minority Tory government which would last until 28 January 1886, himself assuming the role of Foreign Secretary. The most notable factor in his government was the sensational entry into the cabinet as Secretary of State for India of Lord Randolph Churchill (1849-95), at the age of just 36. Sir Michael Hicks Beach became Chancellor of the Exchequer and Leader of the Conservative Party in the House of Commons. Most of the other cabinet posts were filled by men who had served in previous Tory governments. Lord Lieutenant of Ireland, an extremely important post at the time, went to Lord Carnarvon. The cabinet still featured eight peers.

The government's tenure was of course a precarious one, dependent upon avoiding parliamentary defeat, an event that would necessitate a general election. Its continued existence relied, therefore, to a large extent, on its approach to Ireland. Usually, a Tory government would take a hard line towards Ireland and would have no truck with Irish nationalism. This government, however, eschewed such an approach, sponsoring a land purchase scheme. The Purchase of Land Act 1885 – also known as the Ashbourne

Act, after its sponsor, Lord Ashbourne (1837-1913) – went further than the agreement between Gladstone and Parnell in the Kilmainham Treaty, setting up a £5 million fund and permitting any tenant who wished to buy land to do so. This could be done by borrowing from the government and paying back the loan in monthly instalments at a fixed rate of interest of four per cent. This ensured that the payments would be affordable. Meanwhile, the Tories stayed close to the Irish nationalists, holding secret talks with the leaders, including Charles Parnell, although nothing significant emerged from them.

Parliament was dissolved in November 1885 for a general election which would be the first since the Third Reform Act had added a substantial number of voters to the electorate. There were a number of important factors at play. The Liberals were divided, Joseph Chamberlain representing the left of the party and appealing to the working class with what was called his 'Unauthorised Programme'. His colleague, Jesse Collings (1831-1920), who had also been Mayor of Birmingham, was proposing that all agricultural labourers be given three acres and a cow, which became the slogan for all those seeking land reform and battling rural poverty. (Three acres and a cow were acknowledged as providing sufficient for a family to live on.) The right, however, consisting of Whigs and moderates, felt uncomfortable with the direction in which the party seemed to be headed. The Liberals were favourites to win the election and Gladstone had worked hard to manage Chamberlain's expectations in the event.

One of the biggest surprises of the election was the fact that Parnell and the Irish Nationalists threw their support behind the Conservatives. In the election, the Conservatives performed well in urban areas, while, probably because of Chamberlain and Collings' efforts on behalf of agricultural labourers, the Liberals gained success in rural constituencies. In the end, the Liberals took 319 seats, the Conservatives 247. There were some independent wins and Parnell's Irish Parliamentary Party won 86 seats, a gain of 23. Parnell's success took the shine off what appeared to be a substantial victory for Gladstone as it meant that he would be leading what was, in effect, a minority government. On 1 February 1886, the 76-year-old Gladstone put together his third government but it would be in office just six months. Sir William Harcourt (1827-1904) was appointed Chancellor of the Exchequer; the 38-year-old Lord Rosebery (1847-1929), the great hope of the moderate wing of the party and a Gladstone loyalist, was given the job of Foreign Secretary. The future Liberal Prime Minister Sir Henry Campbell-Bannerman (1836-1908) was Secretary for War. The cabinet still contained a number of peers – six of them against eight commoners.

Although he had at no point said so in the 1885 election campaign, Gladstone had become convinced that Home Rule for Ireland was a necessary thing to ensure the future stability of British politics. The policy change emerged in an interview that became known as the 'Hawarden Kite'. This was given to the *Leeds Mercury* on 17 December 1885, during the election campaign, by Gladstone's son, Herbert at the family estate at Hawarden in Flintshire in Wales. It is unknown if Gladstone was behind this 'leak' or whether it was purely the press seeking a scoop. As a result of it, the Irish Parliamentary Party withdrew its support from the Tories and put it behind Gladstone.

Home Rule for Ireland was now the overarching issue of British politics. Gladstone was concerned that, if Ireland were to achieve it, the Irish should remain loyal to the Union and to the Crown. After all, a number of colonies had been given self-government and they had retained Victoria as head of state. He believed Ireland should be no different. It was also to be hoped that the violence that was destroying communities in Ireland would cease.

What made this few months so important to the future of British politics was a notion that Lord Randolph Churchill came up with. He decided that, if Gladstone pushed for Home Rule, then the Orange question should be brought into play. In other words, what about Ulster? He coined the slogan, 'Ulster will fight, Ulster will be right'. He also invented the term 'the Unionist party' as an umbrella term for all of the forces opposed to Home Rule, whether they were Tories or Liberals.

In scenes unprecedented in parliamentary history,

Gladstone's first Home Rule Bill was introduced in Parliament on 8 April 1886. There had already been problems when he had first proposed it to his cabinet. Joseph Chamberlain and Sir George Trevelyan (1838-1928), Secretary for Scotland and a radical like Chamberlain, resigned. Chamberlain insisted that Home Rule 'would lead in the long run to the absolute national independence of Ireland'. He added that he believed that would cause Britain to 'sink to the rank of a third-rate power'.

The bill provided for a unicameral assembly that was deliberately not called a 'parliament' because that would draw associations with the Irish Parliament that had been abolished in the 1800 Act of Union. The so-called First Order would be made up of 28 Irish peers plus 75 elected members, albeit chosen by a very limited electorate, and it would have the power to delay legislation for three years. The Second Order would consist of 204 or 206 members, depending on how many members were to be elected by the University of Dublin. Irish MPs would not attend the Westminster Parliament. The Lord Lieutenant of Ireland would retain executive power and he and his executive would not be responsible to the two Orders. Britain would retain control of defence, war, treaties, trade and coinage. One fifteenth of the taxes levied in Ireland was to go to the United Kingdom and the remainder was to be used by the Irish assembly as it wished. Gladstone also devised an ambitious scheme to buy out every Irish landlord, costing the government £120 million.

Feverish debate raged for weeks in Parliament, Lord Salisbury in the Lords, at one point declaring that the Irish, 'like the Hottentots', were 'incapable of self-government'. Ultimately a rebellion against the bill was required by at least 50 Liberal MPs if it was to be defeated. The vote took place on 8 June 1886 and 93 Liberals – known henceforth as Liberal Unionists – sided with the Conservatives to defeat the second reading of Gladstone's bill overwhelmingly. The Prime Minister immediately declared a general election.

It was a decisive moment in British political history. Since 1832, the left-of-centre Liberal Party had been led by peers and its ranks contained many wealthy businessmen. Now, such men drifted towards the Tories as Liberal Unionists, and the Conservative Party began to take on the mantle of the 'establishment' party, made up of the landed aristocracy and the upper middle classes of the south of England. This split in Liberal ranks handed electoral victories to the Conservatives for the next 20 years, and arguably, throughout the next century. The Liberals, for their part, moved further to the left.

Meanwhile, the issue of Ireland remained in abeyance, but, importantly, Ulster was now viewed as a separate entity, with deep-seated consequences for Ireland and for Britain that remain unresolved to this day.

Salisbury's Second Premiership

The election took place in July 1886, just seven months after the last, the shortest period between general elections in modern history. After a campaign in which anti-Catholicism was to the fore, the results in the previous poll were reversed. The Conservatives, led by Lord Salisbury in an electoral pact with the Liberal Unionists, led by Lord Hartington, and Joseph Chamberlain, won 316 seats and the Liberal Unionists took 79. The number of seats won by the Liberals fell dramatically, from 319 to just 192. They had been in power for eighteen of the previous twenty-seven years and had come out on top in five of the six elections held during that time. In the next nineteen years, they would only hold office for three.

Salisbury, taking the office of Prime Minister for the second time, included familiar faces in his cabinet, Northcote as Foreign Secretary, and Hicks Beach in the important role of Chief Secretary for Ireland. He would be replaced the following year by the future Prime Minister, Arthur Balfour (1848-1930) who was Salisbury's nephew. It came as a great surprise to many when Lord Randolph Churchill, still just 36, was made Chancellor of the Exchequer and Henry Matthews (1826-1913), a Roman Catholic, and an ally of Chamberlain, was appointed Home Secretary. There were seven peers and seven commoners in Salisbury's cabinet.

Parnell's star had fallen somewhat through his association with Gladstone and the cause of Home Rule now lay in the hands of two more radical Irish MPs, William O'Brien (1852-1928) and John Dillon (1851-1927). They organised more protests against high rents and evictions in Ireland, and Salisbury replied in 1887 with a Criminal Law and Procedure (Ireland) Act which allocated greater powers to the authorities in Ireland. Devised by Balfour, this legislation gave him the nickname 'Bloody Balfour' as the result of the act was more violence. However, he also passed another Land Act that made a further £33 million available for the purchase of land by tenants. Unfortunately, it took five years to come into effect.

Salisbury's Chancellor of the Exchequer was now the Liberal Unionist George Goschen. Lord Randolph Churchill had tried to slash the budget allocated to the Army and Navy, to the great alarm of his fellow Conservatives. Faced by this opposition, he drafted a resignation letter, confident that Salisbury and the cabinet would reject it and agree to his cuts. His gamble failed, however, and his resignation was accepted. His political career entered a *cul de sac* from which it never again emerged and he died, aged just 45, in 1895. Goschen cut income tax and did not slash military spending in the way that Churchill had planned to. There was reform of local government in England, Wales and Scotland in 1888. County councils were introduced and towns with populations greater than 50,000 also had to have a council. The London County Council was established, although the Corporation and Lord Mayor of the City of London were not altered by the legislation. The new councils were given the power to raise revenues through rates and were made responsible for education, welfare and policing. This began the process of diminishing the authority of local aristocracy and landowners in rural areas, and putting power into the hands of the local council officials.

Literature in the 1880s

Reading, in the late eighteenth and early nineteenth centuries, was a skill enjoyed only by the upper classes and the elite. Furthermore, books were expensive and only the well-off could afford them. At the start of the nineteenth century, it was not unusual for someone to be able to read but not to write. There were undoubtedly financial reasons for this as paper was expensive and the writing implement was a quill pen which made writing difficult and slow. Newspapers were read out loud in public houses and if there was a literate family member, his or her skills would be used to read out loud books or journals.

In the 1830s, a new popular form of writing began to appear – prose fiction broken down into weekly parts and sold for one or two pence. They were usually sensational stories, often with Gothic elements, and they often did not have an ending, merely carrying on until readers tired of them and moved on to another story. Later, in the 1850s and 1860s, a story could be serialised over a number of years. The fact that such stories were being published in ever increasing numbers was evidence of the growth of literacy in the country, growth that was helped by the Forster Education Act of 1870 that had supported compulsory, free education for children.

Victorian novels were, more often than not, published in three volumes. These were dubbed 'triple-deckers' and cost ten shillings and sixpence a volume, the money made from the first volume often subsidising the production of the second. If that was too expensive for a lot of people, there were lending libraries to supply their needs for a fee. Eventually, the government funded public libraries which were much cheaper and were available to a greater percentage of the population. Railway journeys provided a good environment in which to read and the publisher Routledge launched the Railway Library in 1849. Books cost a shilling per volume and the venture was hugely successful, having published 1,277 volumes by 1898 when it closed.

Charles Dickens was one of the authors who tried to change the triple-decker novel system, publishing stories on a monthly basis and charging one shilling per instalment. These did have definite endings and would appear in about 20 parts. Ultimately, this allowed the reader to enjoy a novel for one pound rather than 31 shillings and sixpence. Around the text of the novel there would be adverts, news reports and reviews of the latest books. By the end of the nineteenth century, a newly literate working-class population had access in many different ways to books of which their antecedents could only have dreamed.

A triple-decker, published in 1880, was George Gissing's (1857-1903) first novel *Workers in the Dawn*, focusing on the unhappy marriage of an artist called Arthur Golding and a prostitute, Carrie Mitchell. Gissing wrote that it was an 'attack upon certain features of our present religious and social life which to *me* appear highly condemnable'. The Irish writer George Moore's (1852-1933) novel of 1883, *A Modern Lover*, was published in three volumes to satisfy the circulating or lending libraries that were all-powerful in the book world at the time. Unfortunately, libraries such as Mudie's Select Library, one of the largest and most influential, banned the book because of the amorous adventures of the book's hero. This, of course, created huge publicity and equally huge sales, especially for his next book, *A Mummer's Wife* in 1885, which was also banned by WH Smith but reached its fourteenth edition during its first year of publication.

In 1887, the most celebrated fictional detective of them all, Sherlock Holmes, first appeared in print in *A Study in*

Scarlet which was published in *Beeton's Christmas Annual*. When the stories of the detective and his trusty assistant, Dr Watson, began to appear in *The Strand Magazine* in 1891, the character became a phenomenon.

Treasure Island, the Scottish author Robert Louis Stevenson's (1850-94) much-loved 1883 tale of pirates and treasure, was originally serialised in the children's magazine *Young Folks* in 1881 and 1882. It is enjoyed for its atmosphere, action and splendid characters, such as Long John Silver, Billy Bones, Blind Pew and Jim Hawkins. He would follow that in 1886 with *The Strange Case of Dr Jekyll and Mr Hyde*, the story of a London lawyer, Gabriel John Utterson, who investigates strange occurrences involving his friend, Dr Henry Jekyll and the evil Mr Hyde. Initially sold for a shilling in paperback, it was one of the earliest so-called 'shilling shockers' and sold 40,000 copies in the first six months of publication. Stevenson's historical adventure novel, *Kidnapped*, also appeared in 1886, again initially serialised in *Young Folks*. It has been admired by writers as diverse as Henry James, Jorge Luis Borges and Hilary Mantel. Another fantastic story – that of King Arthur – was told by Alfred, Lord Tennyson in a cycle of 12 narrative poems, *Idylls of the King*, which were published between 1859 and 1885. This epic poem is often read as an allegory for the conflicts in society in Victorian Britain.

Before becoming a well-known playwright in the 1890s, Oscar Wilde (1854-1900), an Irish writer living in London, experimented with writing in various forms in the previous decade. He was the leading exponent of what was described as 'decadence', an aesthetic also pursued by the illustrator and author, Aubrey Beardsley (1872-98), the poet and critic, Arthur Symons (1865-1945) and the poet and novelist, Ernest Dowson (1867-1900). Decadents espoused pessimism over optimism, decay over life and embraced the abnormal. There were suspicions that they indulged in drug-taking and homosexuality, and they were generally viewed as corrupting influences. In fact, in the Criminal Law Amendment Act of 1885, homosexual activity was, for the first time, classified as gross indecency, whether in public or in private. The same legislation raised the age of consent for girls from 13 to 16.

7

The 1890s:
Towards the End of an Era

Leisure and entertainment in the Victorian Era

Leisure time was a fairly alien concept to most Victorians but, as the nineteenth century progressed, things improved. In 1871, the Bank Holiday Act established bank holidays in the United Kingdom for the first time. There were four of them in England, Wales and Ireland – Easter Monday, Whit Monday, the first Monday in August and Boxing Day (England and Wales) and St Stephen's Day (Ireland). Scotland had five – New Year's Day, Good Friday, the first Monday in May, the first Monday in August and Christmas Day. Good Friday and Christmas Day were viewed in England and Wales as traditional days of rest, like Sundays. Often, even towards the end of the century, Sundays and Bank Holidays were the only paid holidays most people had, although in the 1870s, some clerks and skilled workers began to be given a week's paid holiday. The half-day off on Saturday stipulated in the 1847 Factory Act became the norm for most workers in the 1890s, introducing the notion of the weekend.

The issue was, of course, how that spare time enjoyed by most was going to be filled. One way that gained popularity at the time was to play or watch sport. It was during the nineteenth century that most sports became organised with formal sets of rules and regulations that were adhered to by all participants. Rugby's rules were drawn up at Rugby school in 1845 and the Rugby Football Union, the governing body of the sport to this day, was founded in 1871. The Home Nations Championship – the precursor of today's Six Nations Championship – was first competed for in 1883. The rules for boxing were drawn up in 1867 by the Welsh sportsman, John Graham Chambers (1843-83). These – often known as the Marquess of Queensberry Rules – made it mandatory for boxing gloves to be worn and introduced the count to ten and the three-minute round. The rules of football were devised by the London Football Association in 1863, and the Amateur Athletics Association was founded in 1880.

Many sports developed through the centuries and were codified in the nineteenth; other new sports were invented, such as lawn tennis. A form of tennis had been played in Europe since the Middle Ages but the modern version was developed and popularised by the British army officer,

Walter Clopton Wingfield (1833-1912), amongst others, around 1873. Snooker originated amongst British army officers in India in the second half of the nineteenth century, and the first set of rules was created by the army officer Sir Neville Chamberlain (1856-1944). The word 'snooker' was used to describe first-year cadets, but Chamberlain employed it to describe a poor performance at the table.

The invention of the safety bicycle in 1876 by English engineer, Harry Lawson (1852-1925) made cycling a sport that could be enjoyed by all. With this cycle, the rider's feet were within reach of the ground, rendering it easier to stop, unlike the penny-farthing, for instance, where the rider was seated high above the ground. Cycling and cycling clubs rapidly became extremely popular, especially after the invention of the pneumatic tyre by Scottish inventor, John Boyd Dunlop (1840-1921), in 1892. For the first time, people who did not own horse-drawn vehicles could buy a bike and travel fairly long distances. And they did in their thousands, including many working-class women. One woman cyclist reported in 1899 that:

'The bicycle is in truth the women's emancipator. It imparts an open-air freedom and freshness to a life hithertofore cribbed, cabined and confined by convention. The cyclists have collided with the unamiable Mrs Grundy [a figurative name for a very conservative person] and ridden triumphantly over her prostrate body.'

Other leisure pursuits included the music hall which became increasingly popular as the century passed and reading which are both discussed elsewhere in this book. Photography, too, became popular, and the English scientist and inventor, Henry Fox Talbot was one of its pioneers.

The first public parks began to be laid out by town councils and others in the nineteenth century. One of the earliest was Princes Park in Toxteth in Liverpool. Designed by Joseph Paxton (1803-65), later to be the designer of the Crystal Palace, it opened in 1843. The first public playground built for children was created in a park in Manchester in 1859.

The 'modern' Christmas, with Christmas trees and cards, was largely a Victorian invention. Until then, it was merely one more religious festival amongst many but Christmas Day became a holiday in 1834 and Boxing Day was added in 1871. A major contributor to the development of Christmas as an important holiday was Charles Dickens's phenomenally popular book, *A Christmas Carol*. He made it a family-focused festival of generosity. The words 'Merry Christmas' came from the book. Sir Henry Cole invented the Christmas card in 1843 and the Christmas tree arrived early in the century and was popularised by Queen Victoria and Prince Albert.

The 'Long Depression'

The slump that followed the boom of the middle of the century was known to the Victorians as the 'Great Depression' although it has come to be known as the 'Long Depression'. It affected not just Britain, but the whole world, although Europe and the United States felt it worst. It perhaps had the most impact in the United Kingdom where it lasted from 1873 to 1896. Britain experienced the slowest economic growth since the industrial revolution and it put a dent in the view that Britain's prosperity was permanent. Unemployment was very high during some years in the late 1870s and also in 1886-87 and 1893-94. There was a downturn in prices which, at least, had the benefit of bolstering spending by the working class on consumer goods. This came about because of the fall in prices for agricultural goods which had resulted from the globalisation of the market for meat and arable crops. Rural communities were hit very hard by this and the profits made by farmers plummeted, as did the rents that landlords could levy. This, in turn, brought down the value of land. Migration from the countryside to towns – already significant – increased as a result and the countryside would suffer from a deep depression from this time until after the Second World War. It seemed that the critics of Peel's repeal of the Corn Laws had possibly been right, and the price of British-grown wheat had fallen and would remain low for the rest of the nineteenth century. By 1885, the amount of land devoted to growing it had reduced by a million acres and land devoted to barley had also diminished. In the 1830s grain imported to Britain was 2 per cent of the total consumed; in the 1860s it was 24 per cent; and by the 1880s it was 45 per cent, 65 per cent for wheat alone. The number of farm workers fell commensurately. The 1881 census showed more than 90,000 fewer while urban labourers increased by more than 53,000, presumably farm workers who had moved to the towns and cities to find work. Between 1871 and 1911 agriculture's contribution to the British economy fell from 17 per cent to less than 7 per cent. It is worth reminding ourselves that Disraeli, although a supporter of the Corn Laws who predicted catastrophe for agriculture if they were repealed, failed, when in government, to introduce tariffs on imported goods, while all other European powers did just that.

Meanwhile, Britain based its future on being the 'workshop of the world'. But that, too, faced challenges. At the start of the 1890s, Germany and the United States were rapidly gaining ground, not just in industrial output but in innovation, too. By the end of the decade, Germany had moved ahead of Britain. This had been foreseen by the Royal Commission on the Depression in Trade and Industry that had reported on the situation in 1886. The commission noted the success of the Germans and reported on the intense competition that Britain was facing. However, with a free-trader as chairman, it was never going to stray from free-trade orthodoxy, even in the face of calls from many Tories for protection for British industry. Britain insisted on staying true to its free-trade philosophy which resulted in the country being flooded with cheap goods manufactured abroad while exports suffered through the tariffs being placed upon them by the United States and other nations.

At the same time, although many were experiencing a better life, there were also many living in deplorable conditions. The 1885 Royal Commission on the Housing of the Working Classes reported on terrible overcrowding amongst the poorly paid. It had been revealed in the 1881 census that 10 per cent of the population was living more than two to a room, a figure that rose to 20 per cent in the capital. Another Royal Commission, looking at labour between 1891 and 1894, found that the average annual earnings of an adult male manual worker in 1885 had been just £60 and over 80 per cent of this group earned no more than 30 shillings per week. Another investigation in 1895 reported that the number of elderly people who had to enter workhouses to survive was on the increase.

Salisbury on the Wane

In the early 1890s, Salisbury's government abolished fees for elementary education and created a Board of

Agriculture. Furthermore, in the 1891 Factory Act, the age at which children could be employed in factories was raised from ten to eleven years of age and women could not be employed within four weeks of giving birth. Despite this, the government's popularity was falling in the face of the poor performance of the economy and other factors, and normally solid Conservative seats fell in by-elections. Salisbury dissolved Parliament in June 1892 and the general election was held in July.

The Liberals had failed to bring themselves together again, but Gladstone still controlled the party machinery, especially the powerful National Liberal Federation. It was at a meeting of the NLF that a programme of policies was drawn up in 1891. The most important element of the programme – dubbed the Newcastle Programme – was Irish Home Rule, but other policies were included, such as land reform, reform of the House of Lords, shorter parliaments, free education, district and parish councils, voter registration reform and the abolition of plural voting and other matters. This was the first time in UK politics that such a programme was created for use in an election campaign and presaged the way modern political parties operate.

In the election, the Liberals made substantial gains in their number of seats, taking 272, compared to 191 in the last election. The number of Conservative and Unionist MPs fell from 393 to 313 and the Irish Parliamentary Party took 81 seats. Thus, the Conservatives and Unionists had a majority, but the Irish MPs joined together with Gladstone and his party in August of that year and Salisbury was forced to resign.

Gladstone, Prime Minister for the fourth time, was, by this time, 82 years old, the oldest Prime Minister in British history, but his government was only in power because of the support of the Irish MPs. His cabinet was less patrician than had previously been the case, although their Lordships Kimberley and Ripon (1827-1909) and Earl Spencer returned to it, and Lord Rosebery became Foreign Secretary. Sir William Harcourt was Chancellor again while Trevelyan returned to the Scottish Office. The rest were commoners, businessmen and professionals.

The last 18 months of Gladstone's glittering career were devoted, as much of his recent past had been, to the issue of Home Rule. He introduced a second Home Rule Bill in February 1893, delivering one of his magnificent orations. With the help of the Irish Nationalists, it passed its second reading but was heavily defeated in the Lords later that year. It was a defeat that pleased Salisbury, Chamberlain and Queen Victoria who deplored the idea of Home Rule for Ireland. And it marked the end for the Grand Old Man even though he was reluctant to go. Not long afterwards, he entered into another dispute with his disaffected cabinet and was forced to resign, bringing to an end the most extraordinary political career of the nineteenth century and perhaps the most extraordinary ever. Quite predictably, there was trouble even after he had gone. The Queen did not offer him a peerage because she was well aware that he would not accept it and she refused to consult him, as was traditionally the case with a departing Prime Minister, on who should succeed him in office. She chose Lord Rosebery, an aristocrat of the first order, married to a Rothschild and a man of letters. He was a racehorse owner whose horses would twice win the Epsom Derby while he was in office. He was also, however, a difficult man, arrogant and complex. His unhappy government, containing at least two men who thought that they should have been chosen over him, lasted just fifteen months.

The cabinet did not change much and neither did it do much. In 1894, income taxes were raised and a new type of death duty on property was introduced. There was outrage from the usual quarters – the landed gentry and wealthy aristocrats. Rosebery was pretty much an expansionist and Uganda was annexed during his tenure after the British East Africa Company hit financial difficulties. Finally, the government was put out of its misery in June 1895 when it was defeated on a defence issue in the Commons. Rosebery resigned and never held public office again.

The Conservatives' Great Day

Lord Salisbury returned to the fray as Prime Minister for the third time in June 1895. Sensing that the omens were good for the Conservatives, his first act was to call a general election. And, indeed, the omens were very good. It was their greatest election victory since before the Reform Act of 1832. They won 411 seats to the Liberals' 177. The Irish National Federation and the Irish National League won 70 and 12 seats respectively. It was the first time since Disraeli's victory in 1874 that the Conservatives had secured a majority. Seventy Liberal Unionist MPs were returned to Parliament which meant that those opposed to Home Rule now outnumbered those in favour.

Salisbury put together a large cabinet. He took the job of Foreign Secretary again and he would occupy both positions until 1900. His nephew, Arthur Balfour – now nicknamed 'Prince Arthur' – was generally accepted to be Prime Minister-in-waiting. Hicks Beach was once again Chancellor, Sir Matthew White Ridley (1842-1904) was Home Secretary and Lord George Hamilton (1845-1927) was Secretary of State for India. Joseph Chamberlain was appointed Colonial Secretary, and Lord Lansdowne (1845-1927) Secretary of State for War. There were nineteen ministers, of whom ten were peers. A number of the commoners were very much part of the elite – three were close relatives of peers and two baronets.

Lord Salisbury would win again in 1900, making him possibly the most successful leader the Conservative Party had between 1832 and 1918, despite his pessimism about the future and his negativity. He was so successful, of course, partly because of the comparative weakness of the Liberals at the time. Gladstone's obsession with Home Rule for Ireland had not only split his party; it had also turned much of the country against him and the Liberals. To make matters worse, they seemed to have run out of ideas. Nor could they match the Conservatives in funding, and they failed to organise as effectively as their rivals. The Great Depression had also played into Conservative hands. At times such as those – and it occurred again in subsequent decades when there was a financial downturn – the right always prospered. The Tories also championed the British Empire, although Salisbury was not a true imperialist. Importantly, he also realised that there were votes to be had amongst the new professional middle class and organised his party to take advantage of this. The Tory victory in 1900 would confirm that the Conservatives had well and truly won back middle-class hearts.

The Boer War

It would be Joseph Chamberlain, however, who would, stamp his name on the ten years between 1895 and 1905, mainly because of one thing – the Boer War. In 1895, Chamberlain was already 69 years old, but although he was not the leader of his party and, in fact, held only a relatively minor post in the cabinet, he became its most influential member. And there were now two Chamberlains in the government because, following the 1895 election, his son Austen (1863-1937) had become Civil Lord of the Admiralty. Joseph Chamberlain feared at this time for Britain's global supremacy in manufacturing, viewing the move in the economy away from industry and entrepreneurship to banking and commerce as very dangerous for the future of the country. He was concerned at the cost of running the empire, but, ironically, he also wanted to expand British territory. His ambition was to consolidate the British Empire into an unassailable global entity and thereby prevent it from going the way of empires of the past that had fallen into decline and decadence.

The Boer War resulted from more than a century of conflict and disagreement between the Boers of South Africa and Great Britain. It also concerned, however, the substantial deposits of gold that had been found at the Witwatersrand gold mines in 1886. At the time, the southernmost part of Africa was made up of four states – Cape Colony, the Orange Free State, Natal and the Transvaal. Cape Colony had been British since the Anglo-Dutch Treaty of 1814 and, after a short period as an independent Boer republic, Natal had been annexed by Britain in 1843. The two Boer republics of Transvaal and Orange Free State had been created between 1835 and 1856 following the 'Great Trek', the former gaining independence in 1854 and the latter two years later. There were constant battles with indigenous peoples during this time. Everything was changed by the discovery of diamonds in 1867 and gold in 1886. In order to control the diamonds, Britain annexed Griqualand in the Orange Free State in 1871 and six years later the South African Republic, or Transvaal, was also annexed. This lasted just four years before it was taken back by the Boers, led by Paul Kruger (1825-1904) in the First Boer War. From 1880, two British corporations controlled the South African diamond trade – the Barnato Diamond Mining Company and the De Beers Mining Corporation, owned by British businessman, Cecil Rhodes who was also active in politics in Cape Colony. In 1889, Rhodes secured a charter from the British government to set up the British South Africa Company. It was allocated extensive political and economic powers in areas north and east of Transvaal.

The gold rush at the Rand, as Witwatersrand came to be known, brought tens of thousands of fortune-hunters – *Uitlanders*, as the Boers described them – to the region, and they soon greatly outnumbered the Boers. Suddenly, Transvaal became one of the world's wealthiest states, now able to purchase armaments and expertise. The Transvaal also enjoyed a closer relationship with Germany, something of grave concern, of course, to the British government. Rhodes began to goad the Boers, one particularly ignominious incident stirring up a great deal of trouble. He engaged Leander Starr Jameson (1853-1917), an employee of one of his companies, to undertake a raid on the Transvaal. The objective was to encourage an uprising of *Uitlanders* that would overthrow Kruger and his government so that the state could be taken into British control. The Jameson Raid, as it became known, was carried out in December 1895 with a force of around 600 men, including police officers from Rhodes' company and other volunteers. Back in London, Chamberlain tried to stop it, insisting that 'if this succeeds, it will ruin me'. He was unable to do so, although he did prohibit British colonists from providing support to the raiders. Jameson's men were forced to surrender on 2 January 1896, leading the German Kaiser to send a telegram to President Kruger, congratulating him and his government on their success 'without the help of friendly powers', suggesting that Germany would be a potential supporter, if needed. This caused an outbreak of anti-German and anti-Boer sentiment in Britain, and Jameson was treated like a hero. He did, however, spend 15 months in Holloway prison, convicted under the Foreign Enlistment Act of 1870. Chamberlain, meanwhile, denied that he had advance knowledge of the raid. Rhodes was censured by a parliamentary committee looking into the circumstances of the raid, but Chamberlain was cleared of any involvement.

Kruger was re-elected in the Transvaal in 1898 and

continued to crack down on the rights of *Uitlanders*. Several months after the November 1898 murder of an English worker by a Boer policeman, a petition, signed by more than 21,000 Witwatersrand British subjects, was sent to Britain, demanding equal rights for *Uitlanders*. The British government unsuccessfully negotiated with Kruger's government in an effort to extend the franchise in Transvaal and war between the two states seemed inevitable. The British claimed that, as they were in control of Transvaal and Orange Free State, it was illegal to deny British subjects their rights. The Boers claimed, on the other hand, that they had not signed up to British 'suzerainty' in the 1884 treaty. Therefore, it was up to them what rights *Uitlanders* should have. Following an ultimatum to Britain to withdraw forces that were massing on the border, the Second Anglo-Boer War broke out on 12 October 1899, Orange Free State allying with Transvaal in the conflict.

Most people at the time must have thought that Britain would deal very quickly with the recalcitrant Southern African states, but this was not to be the case. In fact, British reinforcements would take several months to arrive and the Boers outnumbered the British force by two to one. Furthermore, Transvaal's new-found wealth had allowed the Boers to buy modern weaponry from France and Germany. They fought on horseback and were excellent marksmen which made them masters of the type of warfare that was ideally suited to the terrain. It would take until 31 May

1902 for the British to defeat their enemy but, at the start of the conflict, as the British awaited reinforcements, there was a series of Boer victories. Sieges were the order of the day and the British found themselves besieged at Mafeking which was situated on the border with Bechuanaland, and at Ladysmith and Kimberley in the Orange Free State. In the week from 10 to 17 December – a week that came to be known as 'Black Week' – Britain lost 2,776 soldiers in the battles of Stormberg, Magersfontein and Colenso.

Action was quickly taken, and the British commander, Sir Redvers Buller (1839-1908) was replaced by the distinguished soldier, Field Marshal Lord Roberts (1832-1914). His Chief of Staff was General Lord Kitchener (1850-1916). By the time Roberts was in position, things were beginning to go Britain's way. Ladysmith was relieved on 27 February and in May, Roberts took the Transvaal's main cities – Johannesburg and Pretoria. Mafeking had been besieged for 217 days by the time it was relieved later that month. The news of this latter success engendered mass celebrations back home and an outbreak of jingoistic patriotism. The Orange Free State was annexed and renamed the Orange River Colony and the Transvaal was annexed as the Transvaal Colony.

That, however, did not bring the conflict to a close. Although Kruger fled to Europe, where he died in 1904, those Boer commanders who remained launched one of the first guerrilla campaigns. There were numerous raids on Cape

Colony during which military posts were attacked and railway lines and telegraph lines were destroyed. Around November 1900, Kitchener, now Commander-in-Chief, forced 120,000 Boer women and children into what became known as 'concentration camps'. More than 26,000 of these prisoners died from the diseases that were prevalent in the terrible conditions in the camps. The Boers were forced to surrender in the face of such brutality but it took until 31 May 1902 for the Treaty of Vereeniging to be signed, officially ending the conflict. By this time, there were 300,000 British troops in Southern Africa and the expenditure had been extraordinary. The army cost £18 million in 1895 but this figure had risen to £61 million by 1900. It is estimated that the Boer War cost Great Britain around £222 million, leading Chancellor Hicks Beach to increase income taxes substantially. Around 22,000 British soldiers lost their lives while the Boers suffered 6,189 military casualties. There were also more than 46,000 civilian casualties, including the women and children who perished in the concentration camps. More than 20,000 indigenous people, interned in separate concentration camps, also died.

Diplomatic Problems and Imperial Expansion

Queen Victoria celebrated 60 years on the throne on 22 June 1897. She had surpassed her grandfather George III on 23 September 1896 as the longest-reigning British monarch in history but asked that any celebrations be held back until the following year when she would celebrate her Diamond Jubilee. Chamberlain came up with the idea of making it a festival of the British Empire and the prime ministers of the self-governing dominions were invited to London. No foreign heads of state were invited, principally to avoid the presence of her grandson Wilhelm II (1859-1941). It was thought that, given the anti-German feeling in Britain at the time, there would be trouble the moment he set foot in the country.

On 22 June, in front of vast, cheering crowds, there was a six-mile procession through the streets of the capital, the Queen being accompanied by troops from every corner of the empire. An open-air service of thanksgiving was held at St Paul's Cathedral, the 78-year-old Victoria seated throughout in her carriage so that she would not have to climb the stairs to the cathedral. There was a naval review at Spithead that featured the greatest number of Royal Navy vessels ever gathered in home waters.

There were tensions between 1895 and 1900, however. The Great Depression had put a dent in Britain's view of itself and abroad there were issues for Britain that made many question whether the British Empire could survive for very much longer. The government became embroiled in diplomatic contretemps with other powers. A border dispute between the colony of British Guiana and Venezuela in 1895 brought problems with the United States. President Grover

Cleveland (1837-1908) invoked the Monroe Doctrine, which stated that no European power should be allowed to take control of any independent state in the Americas, and he announced that an American commission would make a decision on the boundary between the two states without the involvement of Britain. The matter ended with a treaty signed in Washington in 1897 which basically acceded to British wishes, Chamberlain working assiduously behind the scenes to guarantee an amenable result. This was an important moment, marking the beginning of better relations between the two nations, leading eventually to what has been described as the 'special relationship'.

Britain was also having problems with France, enduring a series of territorial disputes in Eastern Africa. Of particular seriousness was the so-called 'Fashoda Incident'. In 1895, Sir Edward Grey (1862-1933), Under-Secretary for Foreign Affairs in the Liberal government shortly before Salisbury came to power, criticised French expansion into territory in the Nile valley claimed by Britain. The French took no notice and their expansion continued. In 1898, a French expedition ventured as far as Fashoda on the White Nile with the objective of taking control of the Upper Nile basin, thus barring Britain's access to Sudan. Lord Kitchener, *en route* with his army to Khartoum, delivered a letter to the French commander, protesting about their presence in the region. There was no fighting and, in fact, the two commanders parted on good terms. When news of this meeting reached Europe, however, it was turned into a major diplomatic incident, and there was a growing clamour for war from both sides. However, realising that a war with Britain would serve no real purpose, the French had withdrawn from the White Nile region by February the following year. They also realised that in the event of a future war with their neighbours Germany, they would have to rely on British support. A war now would make this very difficult. This crisis led, however, to the series of agreements signed between Britain and France in 1904 known as the Entente Cordiale that ensured better relations between the two nations leading up to the First World War.

Meanwhile, in Sudan, the Mahdi died in June 1885, and his successor was Khalifa Abdullah ibn Muhammad (1846-99). As Abdullah had conquered all of Sudan and was expanding into Ethiopia and Egypt, Kitchener, Commander of the Egyptian army, led an expedition into Sudan in 1896. Building a railway line to carry supplies to his troops as he progressed down the Nile, he took Omdurman and Khartoum, defeating the Khalifa. A governor-general, appointed by Egypt with the agreement of the British, took over the running of Sudan which was known as Anglo-Egyptian Sudan until 1956. Effectively, however, it was administered as a Crown colony, a dependent territory under the control of the British government. Ashanti, which was at the time part of the Gold Coast, was taken in

1896, and the British East Africa Protectorate (later Kenya) also became part of the empire around this time.

The High Tide of Conservatism

Chamberlain even exerted influence on the government's domestic agenda. His Workmen's Compensation Act of 1897 was an important achievement for the government, stipulating that accidents at work had to be paid for by the employer. But his former party, the Liberals, were in a mess, lacking strong leadership and policy ideas. The leader of the Liberals in the Commons was Sir William Harcourt who had performed that duty since 1894, while Lord Kimberley, who had held office in every Liberal administration since 1852, led the party in the House of Lords. Harcourt, like Rosebery, was a difficult man, and fell out with his party colleagues over a fairly minor issue in 1898. He resigned and the position went to Sir Henry Campbell-Bannerman who would go on to become Prime Minister between 1905 and 1908. Campbell-Bannerman was opposed to the Boer War and this conflict caused real divisions within the Liberal Party. Many in the party were opposed to the jingoism that surrounded the war and viewed war as something to be undertaken only in self-defence. There were others, however – 'Liberal Imperialists' such as Rosebery, Asquith, Richard Haldane (1856-1928) and Sir Edward Grey – who believed in Britain's imperial aspirations and in bringing European civilisation to non-European cultures. They also viewed with suspicion the progress that the United States and Germany were making. They wholeheartedly supported the action taken by Britain in South Africa. On the opposing side were men such as David Lloyd George (1863-1945), a backbencher who would be Prime Minister during the First World War. This faction was nicknamed the 'Little Englanders' and accused of being pro-Boer. The reality was, for Lloyd George, at any rate, that he viewed the Boers as representing a nation like Wales, which was being bullied by the English. He was joined by many radicals and those of the left, although some, such as the founders of the Fabian Society – George Bernard Shaw and Beatrice Webb who was a close friend of Joseph Chamberlain – were actually in favour of the war. They viewed British imperialism as an opportunity to disseminate democratic forms of governance.

Campbell-Bannerman enflamed passions when he asked in a speech in Bradford: 'When was a war not a war? When it was carried on by methods of barbarism in South Africa.' He intended these words to refer to the concentration camps, but those supportive of the British imperialist agenda claimed that he was calling British soldiers in South Africa barbarians. There was uproar and two people died in a riot during an anti-war speech by Lloyd George in Birmingham on December 1901.

Suddenly, Salisbury surprised everyone by calling a snap general election a couple of years before one was due. He relied on the fact that Britain was recording a decisive victory against the Boers and hoped that a wave of nationalism and patriotism would return the Tories to government. It was described, therefore, as a 'khaki election', a reference to the new colour of the uniforms that British troops in South Africa were wearing. People went to the polls in October 1900 and the result was very close. Nonetheless Salisbury became the first Tory leader for many years to win two successive elections. His party claimed 402 seats, 9 fewer than in 1895, while Campbell-Bannerman's Liberals took 183, an increase of 6. The Irish Parliamentary Party took 77 seats. The Labour Representation Committee – later the Labour Party – fought its first election and succeeded in winning 2 seats, Keir Hardie (1856-1915) taking Merthyr Tydfil and Richard Bell (1859-1930) winning Derby. It was a good showing by the Conservatives, their overwhelming support from the middle classes evident, and they even won a majority of Scottish seats.

End of an Era

There was the unavoidable feeling that the end of the nineteenth century was also the end of an extraordinary period in British history. Britain had dominated the century with its industrial supremacy, its justified claim to be the 'workshop of the world', and the empire that had turned so much of the globe red. There was a nervousness about what the future might hold, as the other major powers caught up with Britain in terms of both industrial power and innovation. The twentieth century might be for others to dominate.

Such morbid thoughts were cast into even greater perspective when the woman who had been ever-present for about the last two-thirds of the century, Queen Victoria, passed away. She had spent Christmas at Osborne House on the Isle of Wight as usual but, by this time, she was suffering badly from rheumatism in her legs and her vision was affected by cataracts. In early January 1901, she complained of feeling unwell and by the middle of the month she said she was 'drowsy... dazed, [and] confused.' At 6.30 on the evening of 22 January, she died, aged 81. She had occupied the throne for 63 years, seven months and two days, a reign surpassed only by her great-great granddaughter, Elizabeth II in 2015. At her deathbed were her son, the Prince of Wales, and her eldest grandson, Emperor Wilhelm II of Germany.

She left detailed instructions for her funeral. Dressed in a white dress and her wedding veil, she was lifted into her coffin three days after her death by Edward VII, the Kaiser and her third son, Prince Arthur, Duke of Connaught (1850-1942). Mementos of family, friends and servants were placed in the coffin with her, along with her husband's dressing gown, a plaster cast of his hand, and a lock of the hair and a photo of her faithful retainer, John Brown. The latter was, apparently, placed in her left hand, hidden by a bunch of flowers, at her request. She was then carried from the Isle of Wight where she had died, to Gosport on board HMY *Albany*. The following day, a train took her to Waterloo station in London. Her casket was then carried on a gun carriage to Paddington station and from there to Windsor Castle by rail. The funeral took place on Saturday 2 February, in St George's Chapel at Windsor Castle, and she was buried alongside Prince Albert at Frogmore Mausoleum in Windsor Great Park.

Victoria had become unpopular during the years following the death of her husband when she declined to appear in public and, at this time, republicanism was very much abroad in the country. Latterly, however, during the 1880s and 1890s, she had become extremely popular, a much-loved figure who, for many, embodied the British Empire and was known as the 'grandmother of Europe'. Much had changed during her time on the throne – the extension of the electoral franchise and the increasing power of the House of Commons diminishing the power of the Lords and the monarchy. She had taken the throne at a time when the monarch could still influence affairs of state, but over the decades, to her dismay, this power diminished. A modern constitutional monarchy was established and that has undoubtedly contributed to the survival of the institution to this day. She created a monarchy that emphasised morality and family values, setting an example to which the growing middle class could aspire. She was the head of the greatest empire in history and was the leading light of Europe's royalty. Indeed, her influence over European royalty has continued to this day and the descendants of the 34 of her 42 grandchildren who survived to adulthood pepper the continent's current royal families. Amongst those are, of course, Elizabeth II, Queen of the United Kingdom (born 1926); Prince Philip, Duke of Edinburgh (born 1921); Harald V, King of Norway (born 1937); Carl XVI Gustaf, King of Sweden (born 1946); Margrethe II, Queen of Denmark (born 1940); and Felipe VI, King of Spain (born 1968).

Victoria had never wanted her son Albert Edward, Prince of Wales to ascend the throne in succession to her. She may have hoped to outlive him, and, indeed, he died just nine years after her. Edward had been a rebel from early on and, as Prince of Wales, had gained a reputation for womanising and indulging in excess. But, he was also charming and undoubtedly intelligent. He was crowned Edward VII at Westminster Abbey on 9 August 1902 and began refurbishing the royal palaces and carrying out many of the duties, such as the State Opening of Parliament, that his mother had ceased to do in her final years. A new age – the Edwardian Era – began.

Further Reading

Black, Jeremy, *Nineteenth-Century Britain*, London: Palgrave, 2002

Cannadine, David, *Victorious Century: The United Kingdom, 1800-1906*, London: Allen Lane, 2017

Harvie, Christopher and Matthew, Colin, *Nineteenth-Century Britain: A Very Short Introduction*, Oxford: Oxford University Press

Matthew, Colin, *The Nineteenth Century (Short Oxford History of the British Isles)*, Oxford: Oxford University Press, 2000

Paxman, Jeremy, *The Victorians*, London: BBC Books, 2009

Rubinstein, WB, *Britain's Century: A Political and Social History 1815-1905*, London: Arnold, 1998

Sweet, Matthew, *Inventing the Victorians*, London: Faber & Faber, 2002

Wilson, AN, *The Victorians*, London: Arrow Books, 2003

Index

256